Table of Contents

2

Directions: Write the name of the animal that answers each riddle.

bear   zebra   monkey   kangaroo

camel   lion   elephant

1. I am big and brown. I sleep all winter. **What am I?** _____

2. I look like a horse with black and white stripes. **What am I?** _____

3. I have one or two humps on my back. Sometimes, people ride on me. **What am I?** _____

4. I am a very big animal. I have a long nose called a **trunk**. **What am I?** _____

5. I have sharp teeth and claws. I am a great big cat. **What am I?** _____

6. I have a huge, strong tail. My baby rides in my pouch as I hop along. **What am I?** _____

7. I like to climb. I eat bananas. I make people laugh. **What am I?** _____

Help the Animals Find Their Cages

Directions: The animals have escaped from their cages! The zookeeper needs your help to get them back where they belong. Draw a line from the animal to the cage with its name on it.

Lion

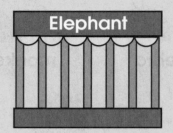

Elephant

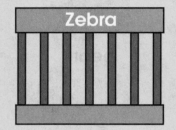

Zebra

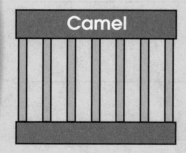

Camel

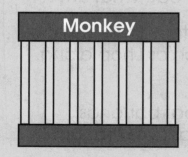

Monkey

Kangaroo

Zoo Animals Word Find

Directions: All the words below are things you might see in a zoo. Find the zoo words hidden in the puzzle. The words can be up, down, or across. Look at the examples.

monkey	tiger	ape
zoo	keeper	cage
snake	giraffe	ostrich
seal	shark	peacock
elephant	bear	zebra
food	emu	moose
lion	fish	bat

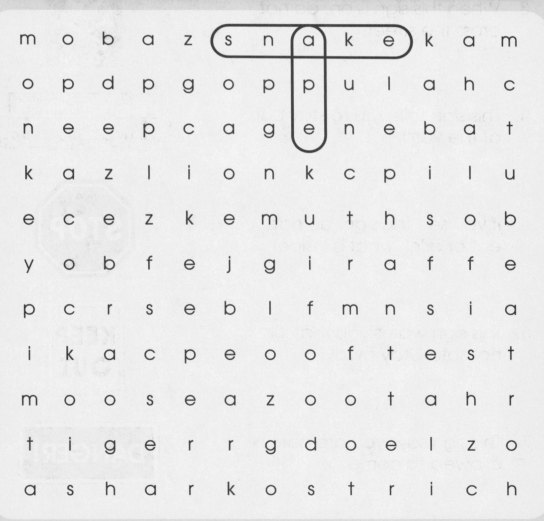

```
m  o  b  a  z  s  n  a  k  e  k  a  m
o  p  d  p  g  o  p  p  u  l  a  h  c
n  e  e  p  c  a  g  e  n  e  b  a  t
k  a  z  l  i  o  n  k  c  p  i  l  u
e  c  e  z  k  e  m  u  t  h  s  o  b
y  o  b  f  e  j  g  i  r  a  f  f  e
p  c  r  s  e  b  l  f  m  n  s  i  a
i  k  a  c  p  e  o  o  f  t  e  s  t
m  o  o  s  e  a  z  o  o  t  a  h  r
t  i  g  e  r  r  g  d  o  e  l  z  o
a  s  h  a  r  k  o  s  t  r  i  c  h
```

Directions: Draw a line from the sign to the sentence that tells about it.

1. If you see this sign, watch out for trains.

2. When cars or bikes come to this sign, they must stop.

3. When this sign is on, do not cross the street.

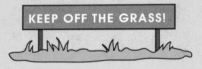

4. This sign tells you to stay out of the yard.

5. If you see this sign, do not eat or drink what is inside!

6. This sign warns you that it is not safe. Stay away!

7. This sign says you are not allowed to come in.

Directions: Read the story about bike safety. Answer the questions below the story.

Mike has a red bike. He likes his bike. Mike wears a helmet. Mike wears knee pads and elbow pads. They keep him safe. Mike stops at signs. Mike looks both ways. Mike is safe on his bike.

1. What color is Mike's bike? _____

2. Which sentence in the story tells why Mike wears pads and a helmet? Write it here.

    _____

    _____

3. What else does Mike do to keep safe?

    He _____ at signs and _____ both ways.

Ordinal Numbers

Directions: Look at the **ordinal words** in the box. Write each word on the correct line to put the words in order.

second	fifth	seventh	first	tenth
third	eighth	sixth	fourth	ninth

1. _____

2. _____

3. _____

4. _____

5. _____

6. _____

7. _____

8. _____

9. _____

10. _____

Directions: Which picture is circled in each row? Underline the correct ordinal word.

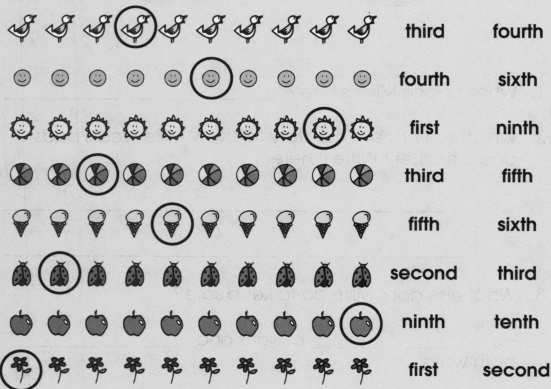

third   fourth

fourth   sixth

first   ninth

third   fifth

fifth   sixth

second   third

ninth   tenth

first   second

Ordinal Numbers

Directions: Look at the pictures. Write the correct ordinal word.

first	second	third	fourth	fifth
sixth	seventh	eighth	ninth	tenth

 _____

 _____

 _____

 _____

 _____

 _____

 _____

 _____

Directions: Read the story about baby animals. Answer the questions with words from the story.

Baby cats are called kittens. They love to play and drink lots of milk. A baby dog is a puppy. Puppies chew on old shoes. They run and bark. A lamb is a baby sheep. Lambs eat grass. A baby duck is called a duckling. Ducklings swim with their wide, webbed feet. Foals are baby horses. A foal can walk the day it is born! A baby goat is a kid. Some people call children kids, too!

1. A baby cat is called a _____ .

2. A baby dog is a _____ .

3. A _____ is a baby sheep.

4. _____ swim with their webbed feet.

5. A _____ can walk the day it is born.

6. A baby goat is a _____ .

Reading for Details

Directions: Read the story about different kinds of transportation. Answer the questions with words from the story.

People use many kinds of transportation. Boats float on the water. Some people fish in a boat. Airplanes fly in the sky. Flying in a plane is a fast way to get somewhere. Trains run on a track. The first car is the engine. The last car is the caboose. Some people even sleep in beds on a train! A car has four wheels. Most people have a car. A car rides on roads. A bus can hold many people. A bus rides on roads. Most children ride a bus to school.

1. A boat floats on the _____ .

2. If you want to get somewhere fast, which transportation

   would you use? _____

3. The first car on a train is called an engine and the last

   car is a _____ .

4. _____ ride on a bus.

5. A _____ has four wheels.

Riddle

Directions: Use the key to match the number with the letter. Write the riddle and the answer.

___ ___ ___ ___   ___ ___ ___   ___ ___ ___
4 19 26 7   23 18 23   7 19 22

___ ___ ___ ___ ___ ___   ___ ___ ___   ___ ___
15 22 7 7 22 9   8 26 2   7 12

___ ___ ___   ___ ___ ___ ___ ___?
7 19 22   8 7 26 14 11

Answer:

___ ___ ___ ___ ___   ___ ___   ___ ___
8 7 18 24 16   7 12   14 22

___ ___ ___   ___ ___   ___ ___ ___ ___
26 13 23   4 22   4 18 15 15

___ ___   ___ ___ ___ ___ ___ ___ ___ ___.
20 12   11 15 26 24 22 24 22 8

Key:

A	B	C	D	E	F	G	H	I	J	K	L	M
26	25	24	23	22	21	20	19	18	17	16	15	14

N	O	P	Q	R	S	T	U	V	W	X	Y	Z
13	12	11	10	9	8	7	6	5	4	3	2	1

Nursery Rhyme Riddles

Directions: Write the name of the character to answer the riddle.

Little Bo Peep   **Little Jack Horner**   **Wee Willie Winkie**

Little Red Riding Hood   **Little Miss Muffet**

1. A spider frightened me! **Who am I?**

   _____

2. You will find me in a corner eating pie. **Who am I?**

   _____

3. A wolf scared me while I was on the way
   to Grandmother's! **Who am I?**

   _____

4. I've lost my sheep. **Who am I?**

   _____

5. I ran through the town in my nightgown. **Who am I?**

   _____

Nursery Rhyme Jumble

Directions: The nursery rhymes are all mixed up! Draw lines to show what the next line should be.

Hint: If you don't know them all, look for rhymes.

Baa, baa, black sheep, •

One, two, buckle my shoe. •

Hickory, dickory, dock. •

Hey, diddle, diddle, •

Jack and Jill went up the hill •

Rub-a-dub-dub, •

Twinkle, twinkle, little star. •

Rain, rain go away, •

Little Miss Muffet •

Little Bo Peep •

• come again another day.

• sat on a tuffet.

• three men in a tub.

• How I wonder what you are!

• the cat and the fiddle.

• to fetch a pail of water.

• have you any wool?

• The mouse ran up the clock.

• has lost her sheep.

• Three, four, shut the door.

Nursery Rhyming Sequencing

Directions: Look at the sentence strips below. Cut out the strips and glue them in the correct order on another piece of paper.

Twinkle, twinkle, little star.

What you are!

 Like a diamond in the sky.

How I wonder

Up above the world so high,

How I wonder

 Twinkle, twinkle little star.

What you are!

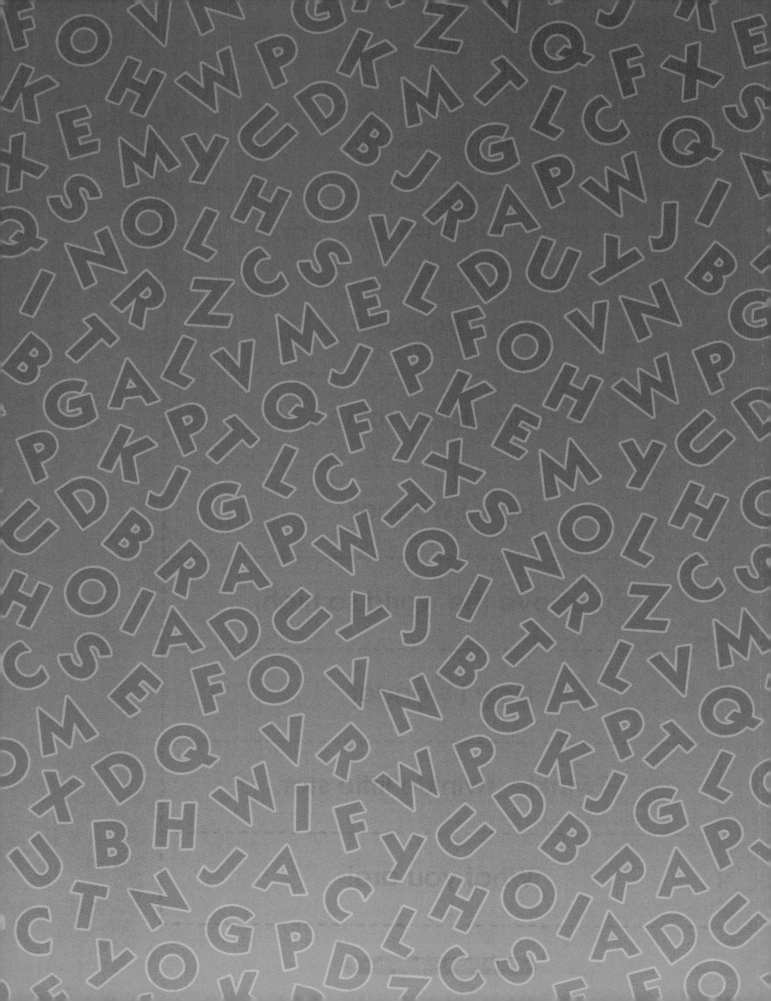

Directions: Write the words from the word box to finish the puzzle.

stop	zebra	Hood	first	
sheep	puppy	elephant	wolf	lamb

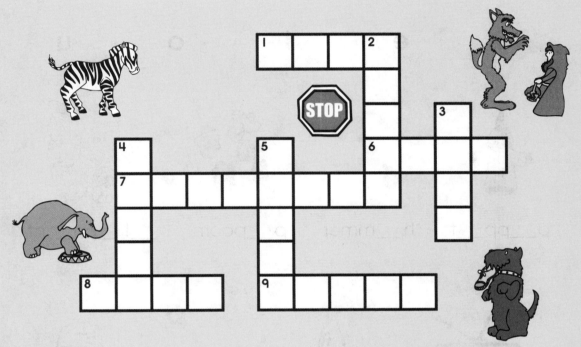

Across:

1. The _____ scared Little Red Riding Hood.

6. The red sign with eight sides means ___.

7. The big animal with the long trunk is the _____.

8. A baby sheep is called a ____.

9. A baby dog is called a _____.

Down:

2. If you are at the front of a line, you are ____.

3. Little Red Riding ____ took a basket of food to her grandmother.

4. The animal that looks like a horse with black and white stripes is the _____.

5. Little Bo Peep lost her _____.

Short Vowels

Vowels can make **short** or **long** sounds. The short **a** sounds like the **a** in **cat**. The short **e** is like the **e** in **leg**. The short **i** sounds like the **i** in **pig**. The short **o** sounds like the **o** in **box**. The short **u** is like the **u** in **cup**.

Directions: Look at the pictures. Their names all have short vowel sounds. But the vowels are missing! Fill in the missing vowels in each word.

a　　e　　i　　o　　u

p___pp___t　　h___mmer　　p___pcorn　　___l___ph___nt

t___l___v___sion　　b___ttle　　sh___v___l　　th___mble

c___ndle　　b___tt___n　　p___nny　　l___dder

Short Vowels

Directions: Cut out the giant vowel letters here and on page 21. Draw pictures or write words with the short vowel sound and put them on both sides of the letters. Then, hang the letters with string!

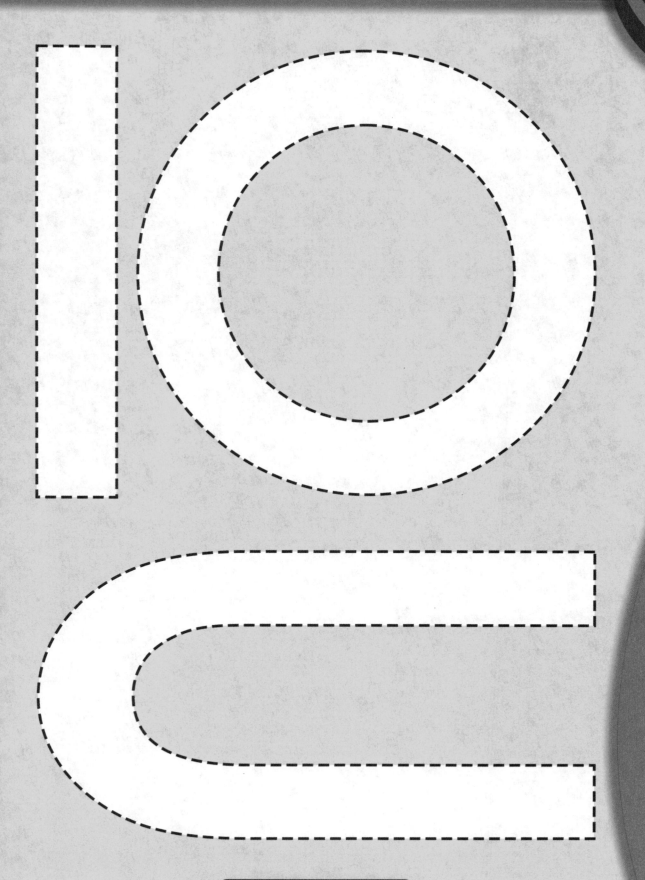

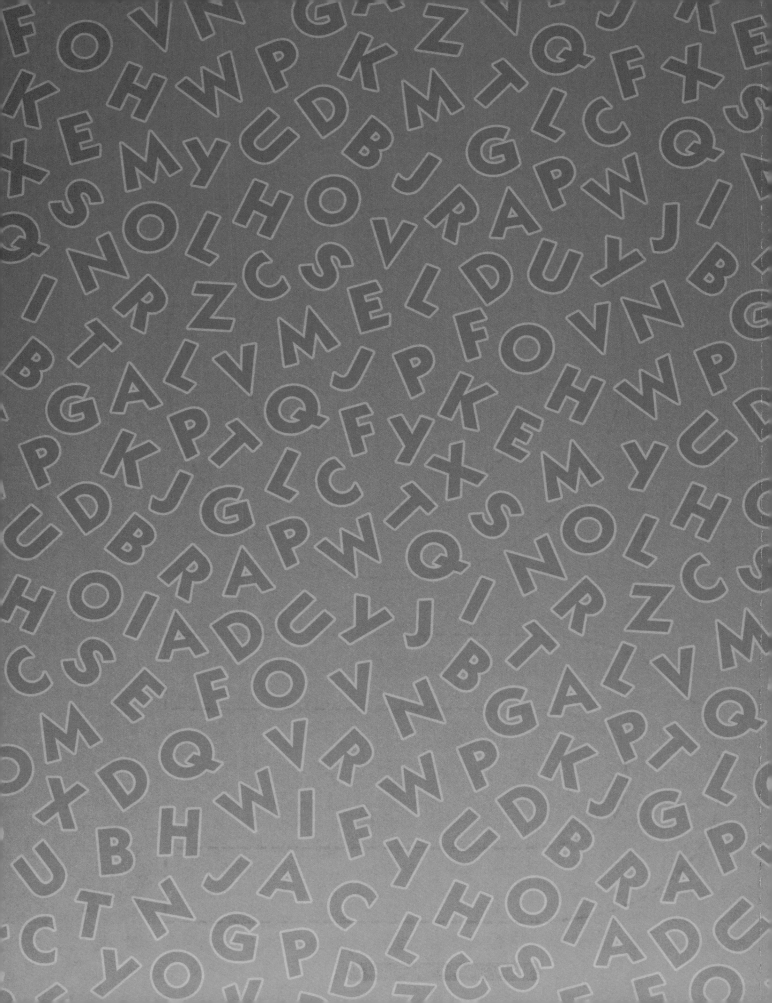

Super Silent e

Long vowel sounds have the same sound as their names. When a **Super Silent e** appears at the end of a word, you can't hear it, but it makes the other vowel have a long sound. For example: **tub** has a **short** vowel sound, and **tube** has a **long** vowel sound.

Directions: Look at the following pictures. Decide if the word has a short or long vowel sound. Circle the correct word. Watch for the **Super Silent e**!

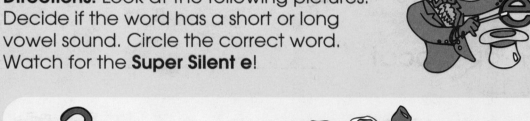

can   cane   tub   tube   rob   robe   rat   rate

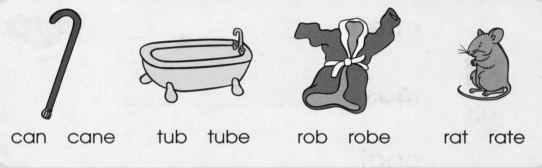

pin   pine   cap   cape   not   note   pan   pane

slid   slide   dim   dime   tap   tape   cub   cube

Double Vowel Words

Usually when two vowels appear together, the first one says its name and the second one is silent.
Example: b**ea**n

Directions: Unscramble the double vowel words below. Write the correct word on the line.

ocat _____

mtea _____

teas _____

ogat _____

atli _____

etar _____

eetf _____

otab _____

spea _____

apil _____

Directions: Read the paragraph. Write the words with the long vowel sounds (**remember:** long vowels say their names) on the lines where they belong. (If a word appears more than once, don't write it again.)

In winter, Jake, Pete, and Bruce like to skate. They go to the lake at the park with other boys and girls. There is one important rule: You must make sure the lake is frozen. Do not skate if the sign reads "ICE NOT SAFE." The park ranger builds a fire for the children to warm their hands. The smoke circles over the pine and spruce trees.

Words with Long a				
J __ __ e	s __ __ e	l __ __ e	m __ __ e	s __ __ e
Words with Long e				
P __ t __ s				
Words with Long i				
l __ e s __ n __		__ e	f __ e	p __ e
Words with Long o				
g __	fr __ n s	s __ __	__ v __ r	
Words with Long u				
B __ __ e	r __ __ e	sp __ __ e		

R-Controlled Vowels

When a vowel is followed by the letter **r**, it has a different sound.
Example: he and **her**

Directions: Write a word from the word box to finish each sentence. Notice the sound of the vowel followed by an **r**.

park	chair	horse	bark	bird
hurt	girl	hair	store	ears

1. A dog likes to _____ .

2. You buy food at a _____ .

3. Children like to play at the _____ .

4. An animal you can ride is a _____ .

5. You hear with your _____ .

6. A robin is a kind of _____ .

7. If you fall down, you might get _____ .

8. The opposite of a boy is a _____ .

9. You comb and brush your _____ .

10. You sit down on a _____ .

Directions: Answer the riddles below. You will need to complete the words with the correct vowel followed by **r**.

1. I am something you may use to eat. **What am I?**

   f _____ k

2. My word names the opposite of tall. **What am I?**

   sh _____ t

3. I can be seen high in the sky. I twinkle. **What am I?**

   st _____

4. I am a kind of clothing a girl might wear. **What am I?**

   sk _____ t

5. My word tells what a group of cows is called. **What am I?**

   h _____ d

6. I am part of your body. **What am I?**

   _____ m

Reading Comprehension

Directions: Read the story. Then, complete the sentences with words from the story.

Mike lives on a farm. There are many animals on the farm: birds, cows, pigs, goats, and chickens. But Mike likes his horse the best. His horse's name is Stormy. Stormy stays in a barn. For fun, Mike rides Stormy to the lake. Stormy helps Mike, too. Stormy pulls a cart to carry weeds from the garden. After a hard day, Mike feeds Stormy corn and hay. For a treat, Stormy gets a pear.

1. Mike lives on a _____ .

2. His favorite animal is a _____ .

3. The horse's name is _____ .

4. Stormy stays in a _____ .

5. It is fun to ride to the _____ .

6. Stormy eats _____ .

Write five words from the story that have an **r-controlled vowel**.

_____ _____ _____

_____ _____

Now, write five words from the story that have a **long vowel sound**.

_____ _____ _____

_____ _____

Hard and Soft c

When **c** is followed by **e, i,** or **y**, it usually has a **soft** sound. The **soft c** sounds like **s. Example: c**ircle and fen**c**e. When **c** is followed by **a** or **u**, it usually has a **hard** sound. The **hard c** sounds like **k. Example: c**up and **c**art

Directions: Read the words in the word box. Write the words in the correct lists. Then, write a word from the word box to finish each sentence. The first one is done for you.

| pencil | cookie | dance | cent | popcorn |
| circus | lucky | mice | tractor | card |

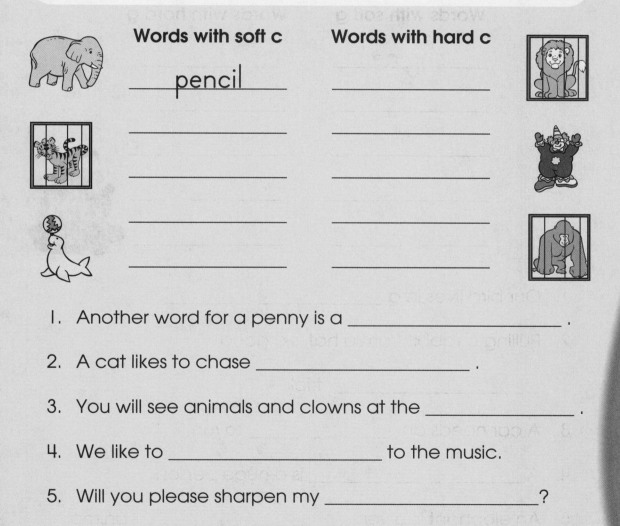

Words with soft c

<u>   pencil   </u>

_____

_____

_____

Words with hard c

_____

_____

_____

1. Another word for a penny is a _____ .

2. A cat likes to chase _____ .

3. You will see animals and clowns at the _____ .

4. We like to _____ to the music.

5. Will you please sharpen my _____?

Hard and Soft g

When **g** is followed by **e, i,** or **y**, it usually has a **soft** sound. The **soft g** sounds like **j. Example:** change and **g**entle. The **hard g** sounds like the **g** in **g**irl or **g**ate.

Directions: Read the words in the word box. Write the words in the correct lists. Then, write a word from the box to finish each sentence. The first one is done for you.

engine	glove	cage	magic	frog
giant	flag	large	glass	goose

Words with soft g	Words with hard g
engine	_____
_____	_____
_____	_____
_____	_____
_____	_____

1. Our bird lives in a _____ .

2. Pulling a rabbit from a hat is a good

   _____ trick.

3. A car needs an _____ to run.

4. A _____ is a huge person.

5. An elephant is a very _____ animal.

Directions: Look at the **c** and **g** words at the bottom of the page. Cut them out and glue them in the correct box below.

soft sound	hard sound

cut ✂ -

jug	giant
grass	grow
juice	engine
gem	crayon
goat	age
face	cart

Y as a Vowel

When **y** comes at the end of a word, it is a vowel. When **y** is the only vowel at the end of a one-syllable word, it has the sound of a long **i** (like in **my**). When **y** is the only vowel at the end of a word with more than one syllable, it has the sound of a long **e** (like in **baby**).

Directions: Look at the words in the word box. If the word has the sound of a long **i**, write it under the word **my**. If the word has the sound of a long **e**, write it under the word **baby**. Then, write the word from the word box that answers each riddle.

happy	penny	fry	try	sleepy	dry
bunny	why	windy	sky	party	fly

my   **baby**

_____   _____

_____   _____

_____   _____

_____   _____

_____   _____

_____   _____

1. It takes five of these to make a nickel. _____

2. This is what you call a baby rabbit. _____

3. It is often blue and you can see it if you look up. _____

4. You might have one of these on your birthday. _____

5. It is the opposite of wet. _____

Vowel Teams

Usually when two vowels appear together, the first one says its name and the second one is silent.

Directions: Find the words in the puzzle. Then, write words from the word box to finish the sentences.

meal	soap	sea	loaf	tail
toe	rain	leaves	coat	toast

```
e  t  o  i  l  s  e  a  p
r  o  a  p  i  o  l  e  d
a  e  r  c  o  a  t  s  m
i  t  t  e  v  p  a  r  e
n  o  a  r  l  i  t  v  a
e  a  i  r  o  l  s  i  l
a  s  l  e  a  v  e  s  t
i  t  e  a  f  e  s  t  r
```

1. Part of your foot is your _____ .

2. Most animals have a _____ .

3. You need an umbrella in the _____ .

4. On a tree you find many _____ .

5. In the bathtub you use _____ .

Vowel Teams

The vowel teams **ou** and **ow** can have the same sound. You can hear it in the words **clown** and **cloud**. The vowel teams **au** and **aw** have the same sound. You hear it in the words **because** and **law**.

Directions: Look at the pictures. Write the correct vowel team to complete the words. You may need to use a dictionary to help you with the correct spelling. The first one is done for you.

_____au_____ to	cl _____ n	h _____ se
fl _____ er	s _____	_____ l
p _____ der	m _____ th	j _____
p _____	m _____ se	cl _____ d

Vowel Teams

The vowel teams **oi** and **oy** have the same sound. You can hear it in the words **oil** and **boy**.

Directions: Finish the sentences by writing the correct word from the word box.

boil	point	coin	boy	toy
joy	join	enjoy	voice	soil

1. You need a pencil with a sharp _____ .

2. A dime is a kind of _____ .

3. Leah's doll is her favorite _____ .

4. The opposite of girl is _____ .

5. To be a member of a club you must _____ .

6. Another word for dirt is _____ .

7. When you talk, we hear your _____ .

8. Ice cream is a dessert I _____ .

9. If water is very hot, it will _____ .

10. Another word for happiness is _____ .

The vowel team **oo** has two sounds. You can remember them with this sentence: Your **foot** goes in your **boot**.

Directions: Look at the pictures. Say their names. If the vowel sounds like the **oo** in **foot**, draw a line to the foot. If it sounds like the **oo** in **boot**, draw a line to the boot.

Vowel Teams

The vowel team **ea** can have a short **e** sound like in **head**, or a long **e** sound like in **bead**. An **ea** followed by an **r** makes a sound like the one in **ear** or like the one in **heard**.

Directions: Read the story. Listen for the sound **ea** makes in the bold words.

Have you ever **read** a book or **heard** a story about a **bear**? You might have **learned** that bears sleep through the winter. Some bears may sleep the whole **season**. Sometimes, they look almost **dead**! But they are very much alive. As the cold winter passes and the spring **weather** comes **near**, they wake up. After such a nice rest, they must be **ready** to **eat** a **really** big **meal**!

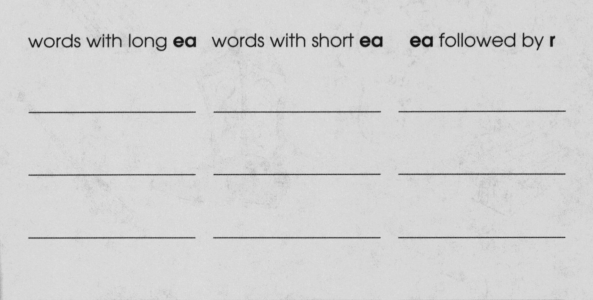

words with long **ea**   words with short **ea**   **ea** followed by **r**

_____   _____   _____

_____   _____   _____

_____   _____   _____

_____   _____   _____

Vowel Teams

The vowel team **ie** makes the long **e** sound like in **believe**. The team **ei** also makes the long **e** sound like in **either**. But **ei** can also make a long **a** sound like in **eight**.

Directions: Circle the **ei** words with the long **a** sound.

neighbor	veil
receive	reindeer
reign	ceiling

The teams **eigh** and **ey** also make the long **a** sound.

Directions: Finish the sentences with words from the word box.

chief   sleigh   obey   weigh   thief   field   ceiling

1. Eight reindeer pull Santa's _____ .

2. Rules are for us to _____ .

3. The bird got out of its cage and flew up

    to the _____ .

4. The leader of an Indian tribe is the _____ .

5. How much do you _____ ?

6. They caught the _____ who took my bike.

7. Corn grows in a _____ .

Vowel Team Scramble

Directions: Unscramble the letters to create words. Draw a picture next to each word.

eamt _____

toab _____

sial _____

mseou _____

cnoi _____

oyt _____

tobo _____

koob _____

brdea _____

leiv _____

Directions: Read the story. Fill in the blanks with words from the word box.

cookies	Joe	bowl	tooth	flour	eight
spoon	eats	enjoys	round	boy	either

Do you like to cook? I know a _____ named

_____ who loves to cook. When Joe has a sweet

_____ , he makes _____ . He puts

_____ and sugar in a _____ and stirs

it with a _____ . Then, he adds the butter and

eggs. He makes cookies that are _____ or other

shapes. He likes them _____ way. Now is the part

he _____ the most: Joe _____ the

cookies. He might eat seven or _____ at a time!

Directions: Fill in the blanks with a word from the word box.

pencil	teacher	crayons
recess	lunchbox	play
fun	math	

1. I need to sharpen my _____ .

2. I like to _____ at recess.

3. School is _____ !

4. My _____ helps me learn.

5. I need to color the picture with _____ .

6. I play kickball at _____ .

7. My sandwich is in my _____ .

8. In _____ I can add and subtract.

Money Words

Directions: Fill in the blanks with a word from the word box.

penny	nickel	dime
quarter	dollar	cent
check	bank	savings

1. Some people call one cent a "lucky _____ ."

2. Mom can write a _____ to buy things.

3. I put some money in my _____ account.

4. Ten cents or a _____ is equal to 10 pennies.

5. One _____ is a penny.

6. I have 100¢ or one _____ .

7. I bought some gum with 25¢ or a _____ .

8. Five cents is also known as a _____ .

9. Make your own sentence using the leftover word.

_____

Days of the Week

Directions: Write the day of the week that answers each question.

Sunday	Monday	Tuesday
Wednesday	Thursday	Friday
Saturday		

1. What is the first day of the week?

   _____

2. What is the last day of the week?

   _____

3. What day comes after Tuesday?

   _____

4. What day comes between Wednesday and Friday?

   _____

5. What is the third day of the week?

   _____

6. What day comes before Saturday?

   _____

7. What day comes after Sunday?

   _____

Directions: Write the name of the month that answers each question.

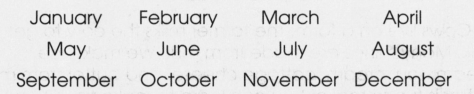

> January   February   March   April
> May   June   July   August
> September   October   November   December

1. Spring starts in the third month. **What is it?**

   _____

2. In some places, school starts the month after August. **What is it?**

   _____

3. Christmas is in the last month of the year. **What is it?**

   _____

4. Summer starts in the sixth month. **What is it?**

   _____

5. Columbus Day is in the month before November. **What is it?**

   _____

6. The second month has the fewest days. **What is it?**

   _____

7. This is the first month of the year. **What is it?**

   _____

Directions: Read the story. Answer the questions. Try the recipe.

Cows Give Us Milk

Cows live on a farm. The farmer milks the cow to get milk. Many things are made from milk. We make ice cream, sour cream, cottage cheese, and butter from milk. Butter is fun to make! You can learn to make your own butter. First, you need cream. Put the cream in a jar and shake it. Then, you need to pour off the liquid. Next, you put the butter in a bowl. Add a little salt and stir! Finally, spread it on crackers and eat!

1. What animal gives us milk?

   _____

2. What four things are made from milk?

   _____   _____

   _____   _____

3. What did the story teach you to make?

   _____

4. Put the steps in order. Write **1, 2, 3, 4** by each sentence.

   _____ Spread the butter on crackers and eat!

   _____ Shake cream in a jar.

   _____ Start with cream.

   _____ Add salt to the butter.

Silly Sentences!

Directions: Cut out the binoculars. Cut out the beginning and ending sentence strips on the next page. Thread the strips through the lenses to make sentences. Write each sentence on a piece of paper. Draw a picture to illustrate your silly sentences. Staple your sentences and illustrations into a book to share.

cut ✄
- -

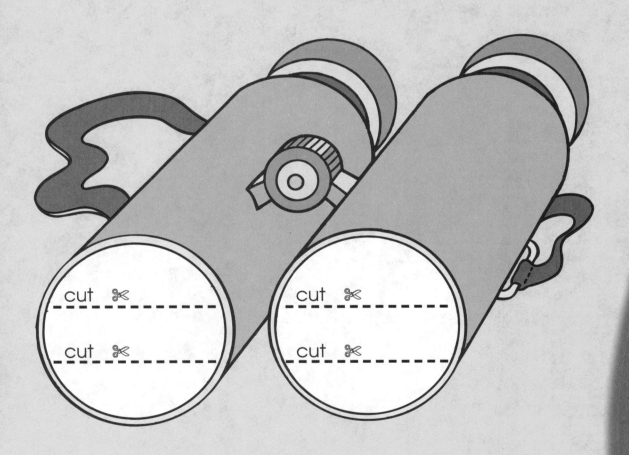

cut ✄

cut ✄

cut ✄

cut ✄

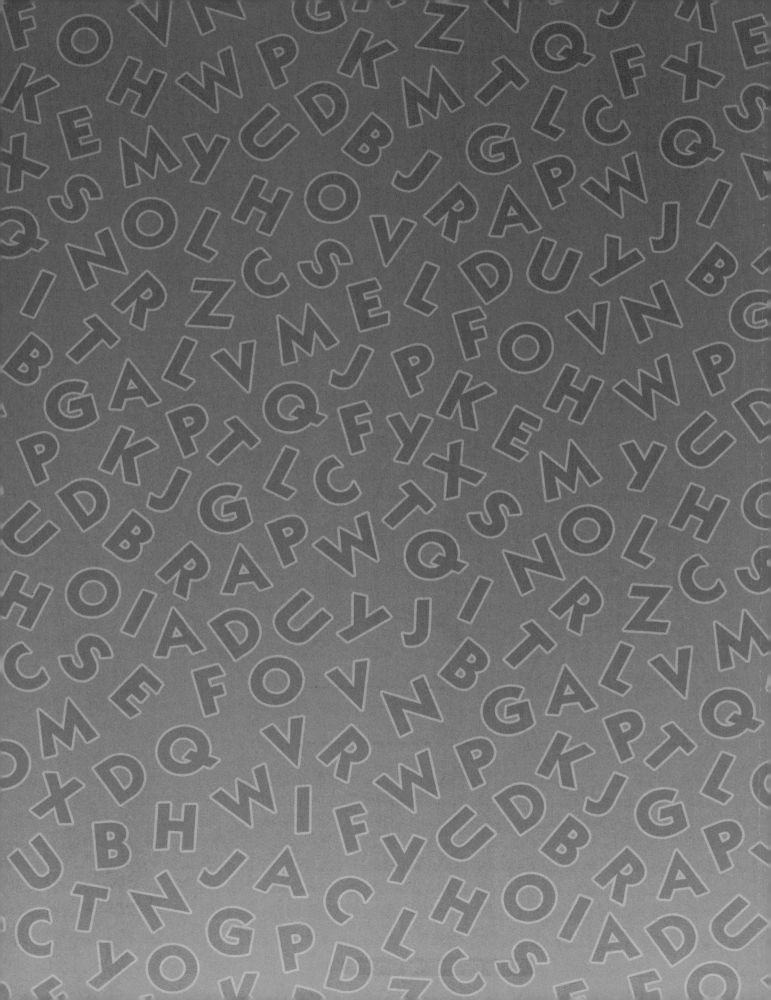

Cats	live in nests.
Boats	read books.
Flowers	have apples.
Birds	smell pretty.
Horses	can slither.
Garbage cans	are playful.
Some trees	smell stinky.
Children	float in water.
Snakes	eat hay.

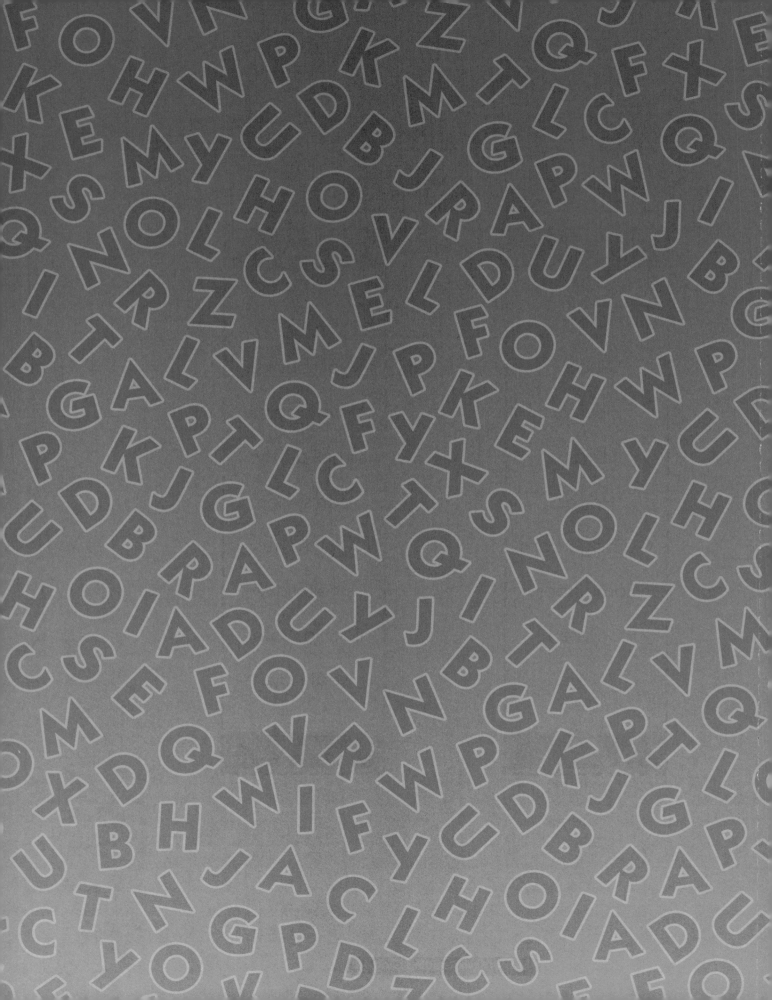

Synonyms

Words that mean the same or nearly the same are called **synonyms**.

Directions: Read the sentence that tells about the picture. Draw a circle around the word that means the same as the bold word.

The child is **unhappy**.

sad   hungry

The flowers are **lovely**.

pretty   green

The baby was very **tired**.

sleepy   hurt

The **funny** clown made us laugh.

silly   glad

The ladybug is so **tiny**.

small   red

We saw a **scary** tiger.

frightening   ugly

Antonyms

Words that mean the opposite are called **antonyms**.

Directions: Read the sentence. Write the word from the word box that means the opposite of the **bold** word.

bottom   outside   black   summer   after
light   sister   clean   last   evening

1. Lisa has a new baby **brother**.   _____

2. The class went **inside** for recess.   _____

3. There is a **white** car in the driveway.   _____

4. We went to the park **before** dinner.   _____

5. Joe's puppy is **dirty**.   _____

6. My name is at the **top** of the list.   _____

7. I like to play outside in the **winter**.   _____

8. I like to take walks in the **morning**.   _____

9. The sky was **dark** after the storm.   _____

10. Our team is in **first** place.   _____

Antonyms and Synonyms

Directions: Find the synonyms and antonyms in the puzzle. Words can be up, down, across, or diagonal.

```
b o k i t t e n o a h l d n
o r e p c o s o f b i g r o
y d g q e a g s f o k p i m
t l v i u c a t o v g i z o
b k a j r i j l d e p q z m
a c f s a l e f t m h r l p
r i g h t o x t b o a t e b
a a l i n w e s a c e y z e
i l o u d a d a s h i p h l
n b n e u d a l l o c u h o
d o g y o o u t s l x p a w
o u u v f c t w p e p p e r
h a m d t o o f u b o y z u
```

Antonyms		Synonyms	
boy	girl	kitten	cat
in	out	big	huge
above	below	dog	puppy
salt	pepper	car	auto
left	right	drizzle	rain
mom	dad	boat	ship
loud	quiet		

Classifying

Classifying is putting similar things into groups.

Directions: Write each word from the word box on the correct line.

| policeman | baby | whale | family | grandfather |
| uncle | goose | fox | kangaroo | donkey |

people   **animals**

_____   _____

_____   _____

_____   _____

_____   _____

_____   _____

Living things need air, food, and water to live. **Non-living** things are not alive.

Directions: Cut out the words on the bottom. Glue each word in the correct column.

Living	Non-living

cut ✂ -

flower	boy
chair	tree
car	ant
book	dog
bread	camera
horse	shoe

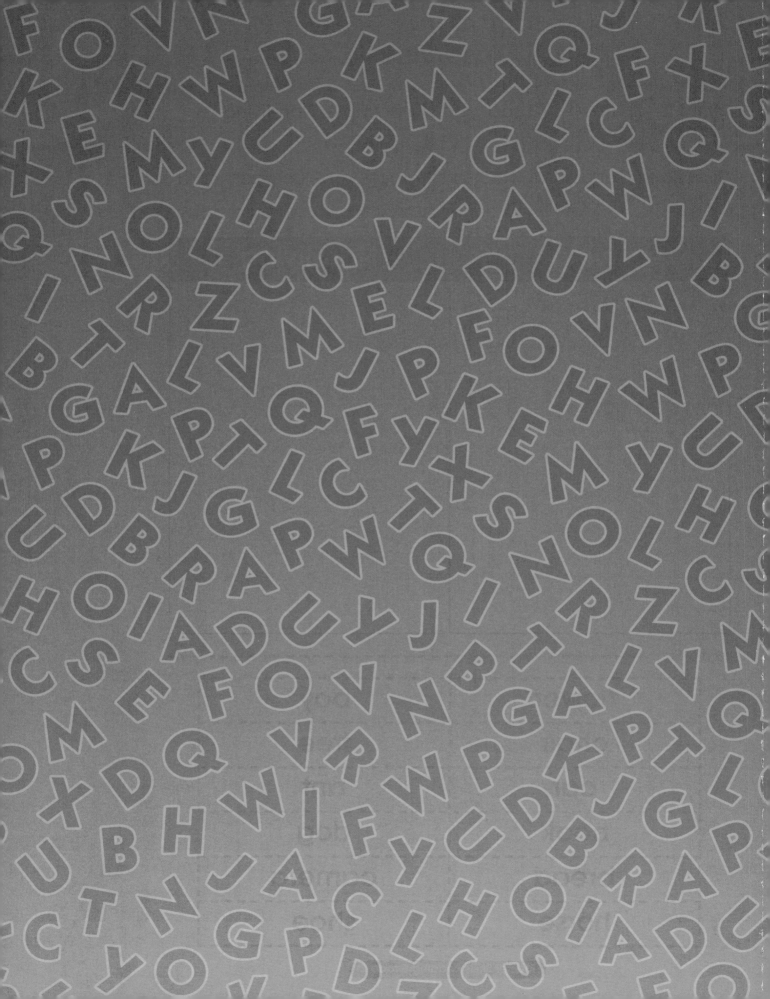

Directions: Read the sentences. Write the words from the word box where they belong.

> bush   rocket   cake   thunder bicycle danger
>
> airplane   wind   candy   rain   car   grass
>
> stop   truck   poison   flower   pie   bird

1. These things taste sweet.

   _____ _____ _____

2. These things come when it storms.

   _____ _____ _____

3. These things have wheels.

   _____ _____ _____

4. These are words you see on signs.

   _____ _____ _____

5. These things can fly.

   _____ _____ _____

6. These things grow in the ground.

   _____ _____ _____

Classifying

Directions: The words in each box form a group. Choose the word from the word box that describes each group and write it on the line.

| clothes | family | noises | colors | flowers |
| fruits | animals | coins | toys |

rose
buttercup
tulip
daisy

_____

crash
bang
ring
pop

_____

mother
father
sister
brother

_____

puzzle
wagon
blocks
doll

_____

green
purple
blue
red

_____

grapes
orange
apple
plum

_____

shirt
socks
dress
coat

_____

dime
penny
nickel
quarter

_____

dog
horse
elephant
moose

_____

Directions: Write the word or words from the word box where they belong.

firetruck   peas   little   speedy   tiny   corn   Saturday
Sunday   rose   potato   short   fast   apple   quick

1. These are words that mean the same as **small**.

   _____

2. These are words that mean the opposite of **slow**.

   _____

3. These things are usually red.

   _____

4. These are vegetables.

   _____

5. The first day of the week is

   _____

6. The last day of the week is

   _____

Compound Words

Compound words are formed by putting together two smaller words.

Directions: Help the cook brew her stew. Mix words from the first column with words from the second column to make new words. Write your new words on the lines at the bottom.

grand	brows
snow	light
eye	stairs
down	string
rose	book
shoe	mother
note	ball
moon	bud

1. _____

2. _____

3. _____

4. _____

5. _____

6. _____

7. _____

8. _____

Directions: Draw a line under the compound word in each sentence. On the line, write the two words that make up the compound word.

1. A firetruck came to help put out the fire.

   _____

2. I will be nine years old on my next birthday.

   _____

3. We built a treehouse in the back.

   _____

4. Dad put a scarecrow in his garden.

   _____

5. It is fun to make footprints in the snow.

   _____

6. I like to read the comics in the newspaper.

   _____

7. Cowboys ride horses and use lassos.

   _____

Contractions are shortened forms of words. An apostrophe is added in place of the letters taken away.

Directions: Help the mother kangaroos find their babies. Draw a line to match the contractions with the words they stand for.

 cannot •   • don't

 is not •   • can't

 will not •   • aren't

 are not •   • won't

 I am •   • couldn't

 could not •   • isn't

 do not •   • I'm

Directions: Match the words with their contractions.

would not •   • I've

was not •   • he'll

he will •   • wouldn't

could not •   • wasn't

I have •   • couldn't

Directions: Make the words at the end of each line into contractions to complete the sentences.

1. He _____ know the answer.   **did not**

2. _____ a long way home.   **It is**

3. _____ my house.   **Here is**

4. _____ not going to school today.   **We are**

5. _____ take the bus home tomorrow.   **They will**

Directions: Write your own contractions in each column below.

Contractions with not	Contractions with will	Contractions with have

Challenge: Write the two words that formed each contraction.

Directions: Cut out the two words and put them together to show what two words make the contraction. Glue them over the contraction.

Similes

A **simile** is a figure of speech that compares two different things. The words **like** or **as** are used in similes.

Directions: Draw a line to the picture that goes with each set of words.

as hard as a •

as hungry as a •

as quiet as a •

as soft as a •

as easy as •

as light as a •

as tiny as an •

Syllables

One way to help you read a word you don't know is to divide it into parts called **syllables**. Every syllable has a vowel sound.

straw•ber•ry

Directions: Say the words. Write the number of syllables.

bird _____   rabbit _____

apple _____   elephant _____

balloon _____   family _____

basketball _____   fence _____

breakfast _____   ladder _____

block _____   open _____

candy _____   puddle _____

popcorn _____   Saturday _____

understand _____   butterfly _____

Syllables

When a double consonant is used in the middle of a word, the word can usually be divided between the consonants.

Directions: Look at the words in the word box. Divide each word into two syllables. Leave space between each syllable. The first one is done for you.

butter	puppy	kitten	yellow
dinner	chatter	ladder	happy
pillow	letter	mitten	summer

but ter

_____   _____   _____

_____   _____   _____

_____   _____   _____

Many words are divided between two consonants that are not alike.

Directions: Look at the words in the word box. Divide each word into two syllables. The first one is done for you.

window	doctor	number	carpet
mister	winter	pencil	candle
barber	sister	picture	under

win dow

_____   _____   _____

_____   _____   _____

_____   _____   _____

Syllables

Directions: Write **1** or **2** on the line to tell how many syllables are in each word. If the word has two syllables, draw a line between the syllables. **Example: supper**

dog _____   timber _____

bedroom _____   cat _____

slipper _____   street _____

tree _____   chalk _____

batter _____   blanket _____

chair _____   marker _____

fish _____   brush _____

master _____   rabbit _____

Review

71

Directions: Circle the word that fits best into each sentence.

1. It is fun to build castles in a ____.

    sandbox   **hatbox**

2. You carry your books in your ____.

    bookbag   **lunchbag**

3. Fall is the best season for playing ____.

    football   **footprint**

4. We ____ ready when our ride came.

    weren't   **he'll**

5. Why ____ my bike be fixed?

    couldn't   **I'm**

6. We ____ see over your head.

    can't   **isn't**

7. This test is as easy as ____.

    pie   **pillow**

8. The baby feels as light as a ____.

    feather   **tree**

Directions: Count the syllables in each word. Write the number on the line. The first one is done for you.

strawberry _____3_____   toenail _____

missing _____   broken _____

understand _____   turtle _____

circle _____   green _____

Directions: Use the key to match the number with the letter. Write the riddle and the answer.

TEE-HEE-HEE!

W H A T   R O O M   H A S
4 19 26 7   9 12 12 14   19 26 8

N O   W A L L S ,
13 12   4 26 15 15 8

TEE-HEE-HEE!

N O   D O O R S ,
13 12   23 12 12 9 8

N O   F L O O R S ,   A N D
13 12   21 15 12 12 9 8   26 13 23

N O   W I N D O W S ?
13 12   4 18 13 23 12 4 8

TEE-HEE-HEE!

Answer:

A   M U S H R O O M !
26   14 6 8 19 9 12 12 14

Key:

A	B	C	D	E	F	G	H	I	J	K	L	M
26	25	24	23	22	21	20	19	18	17	16	15	14

N	O	P	Q	R	S	T	U	V	W	X	Y	Z
13	12	11	10	9	8	7	6	5	4	3	2	1

Consonant teams are two or three consonant letters that have a single sound. **Examples: sh** and **tch**

Directions: Write each word from the word box next to its picture. Underline the consonant team in each word.

bench	match	shoe	thimble
shell	brush	peach	watch
whale	teeth	chair	wheel

_____   _____

_____   _____

_____   _____

_____   _____

_____   _____

_____   _____

Consonant Teams

Directions: Look at the words in the word box. Write all of the words that end with the **ng** sound in the column under the picture of the **ring**. Write all of the words that end with the **nk** sound under the picture of the **sink**. Then, finish the sentences with words from the word box.

| strong | rank | bring | bank | honk | hang | thank |
| long | hunk | song | stung | bunk | sang | junk |

ng

nk

_____ _____

_____ _____

_____ _____

_____ _____

_____ _____

_____ _____

_____ _____

1. _____ your horn when you get to my house.

2. He was _____ by a bumblebee.

3. We are going to put our money in a _____ .

4. I want to _____ you for the birthday present.

5. My brother and I sleep in _____ beds.

Directions: Write a word from the word box to finish each sentence. Circle the consonant teams in your words.

| trash | splash | chain | shut | chicken |
| catch | ship | when | patch | which |

1. My _____ won't lay eggs.

2. I put a _____ on my bicycle so nobody can take it.

3. We watched the big _____ dock and let off its passengers.

4. It is my job to take out the _____ .

5. I have to wear a _____ over my eye until it is better.

6. The baby likes to _____ in the bathtub.

7. Can you _____ the ball with one hand?

8. Please _____ the windows before it rains.

9. _____ are we going to leave for school?

10. I don't know _____ of these books is mine.

Consonant Blends

Consonant blends are two or three consonant letters in a word whose sounds combine, or blend. **Examples: br, fr, gr, pr, tr**

Directions: Look at each picture. Say its name. Write the blend you hear at the beginning of each word.

_____

_____

_____

_____

_____

_____

_____

_____

_____

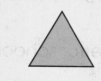

_____

_____

_____

Consonant Blends

Directions: Write a word from the word box to answer each riddle.

clock	glass	blow	climb	slipper
sleep	gloves	clap	blocks	flashlight

1. You need me when the lights go out.
What am I? _____

2. People use me to tell the time.
What am I? _____

3. You put me on your hands in the winter to keep them warm.
What am I? _____

4. Cinderella lost one like me at midnight. **What am I?** _____

5. This is what you do with your hands when you are pleased. **What is it?** _____

6. You can do this with a whistle or with bubble gum. **What is it?** _____

7. These are what you might use to build a castle when you are playing. **What are they?** _____

8. You do this to get to the top of a hill. **What is it?** _____

9. This is what you use to drink water or milk. **What is it?** _____

10. You do this at night with your eyes closed. **What is it?** _____

Consonant Blends

Directions: Blendo the dog needs to fetch his word balls. He needs your help to make the words. Add a blend from the word box to create a word.

br   gr   tr   cl   bl   fl   gl   sl

_____ush

_____ap

_____een

_____ock

_____ock

_____ose

_____uck

_____ip

_____ip

_____oom

_____ag

_____ove

_____ub

_____eep

Directions: Read the words in the box. Write a word from the word box to finish each sentence. Circle the consonant team in each word. **Hint:** There are three letters in each team!

splash	screen	spray	street	scream
screw	shrub	split	strong	string

1. Another word for a bush is a _____ .

2. I tied a _____ to my tooth to help pull it out.

3. I have many friends who live on my _____ .

4. We always _____ when we ride the roller coaster.

5. A _____ helps keep bugs out of the house.

6. It is fun to _____ in the water.

7. My father uses an ax to _____ the firewood.

8. We will need a _____ to fix the chair.

9. You must be very _____ to lift this heavy box.

10. The firemen _____ the fire with water.

Silent Letters

Some words have letters you can't hear at all, such as the **gh** in **night**, the **w** in **wrong**, the **l** in **walk**, the **k** in **knee**, the **b** in **climb**, and the **t** in **listen**.

Directions: Look at the words in the word box. Write the word under its picture. Underline the silent letters.

knife	light	calf	wrench	lamb	eight
wrist	whistle	comb	thumb	knob	knee

_____

_____

_____

_____

_____

_____

_____

_____

_____

_____

_____

_____

Directions: Read the story. Circle the consonant teams (two or three letters) and silent letters in the underlined words. Be sure to check for more than one team in a word! The first one is done for you.

One day last (Spring) my family went on a picnic. My father picked out a pretty spot next to a <u>stream</u>. <u>While</u> my <u>brother</u> and I <u>climbed</u> a <u>tree</u>, my mother <u>spread</u> out a <u>sheet</u> and <u>placed</u> the food on it. But before we could eat, a <u>skunk</u> <u>walked</u> out of the woods! Mother <u>screamed</u> and <u>scared</u> the skunk. It sprayed us with a terrible <u>smell</u>! Now, we <u>think</u> it is a funny <u>story</u>. But <u>that</u> day, we ran!

Directions: Write the words with three-letter blends on the lines.

_____ _____ _____

_____ _____

Directions: Use the key to match the number with the letter. Write the riddle and the answer.

4 19 2   26 9 22   21 18 8 19

8 14 26 9 7 22 9   7 19 26 13

25 18 9 23 8 ?

Answer:

25 22 24 26 6 8 22   7 19 22 2

15 18 5 22   18 13

" 8 24 19 12 12 15 8 ."

Key:

A	B	C	D	E	F	G	H	I	J	K	L	M
26	25	24	23	22	21	20	19	18	17	16	15	14

N	O	P	Q	R	S	T	U	V	W	X	Y	Z
13	12	11	10	9	8	7	6	5	4	3	2	1

Directions: Cut out the scoops of ice cream on the bottom. Glue them on the cones in alphabetical order.

cut ✂ -

lemon dog truck frost

apple house ring

Plurals are words that mean more than one. You usually add an **s** or **es** to the word. In some words ending in **y**, the **y** changes to an **i** before adding **es**. For example, **baby** changes to **babies**.

Directions: Look at the following lists of plural words. Write the word that means one next to it. The first one is done for you.

foxes	_____fox_____	balls	_____
bushes	_____	candies	_____
dresses	_____	wishes	_____
chairs	_____	boxes	_____
shoes	_____	ladies	_____
stories	_____	bunnies	_____
puppies	_____	desks	_____
matches	_____	dishes	_____
cars	_____	pencils	_____

Directions: Circle the word that completes the sentence.

1. Two (cat, cats) played with yarn.

2. The (box, boxes) were all full of clothes.

3. The (wheel, wheels) on my bike was flat.

4. My sister and I each carved a (pumpkin, pumpkins) for fall.

5. The piano has many black and white (key, keys).

6. The five (bunny, bunnies) ate carrots.

7. The dog fetched all the (stick, sticks).

8. I drank a (glass, glasses) of milk.

9. I have five (chair, chairs).

A **suffix** is a syllable added to the end of a word which changes its meaning, as in small, small**er**, small**est**. The word you start with is called the **root word**. Some root words change their spelling before adding **er** and **est**. **Example:** in the word **big**, another **g** is added to make the words big**ger** and big**gest**. In the word **pretty**, the **y** changes to an **i** to make the words prett**ier** and prett**iest**.

Directions: Use words from the word box to help you add **er** and **est** to the root words.

prettier	happier	luckiest	busiest	tinier
luckier	silliest	greener	madder	busier
prettiest	funnier	tiniest	happiest	bigger
biggest	greenest	sillier	maddest	funniest

	er	**est**
happy	_____	_____
busy	_____	_____
tiny	_____	_____
pretty	_____	_____
lucky	_____	_____
big	_____	_____
silly	_____	_____
green	_____	_____
mad	_____	_____
funny	_____	_____

Suffixes

Adding **ing** to a word means that it is happening now. Adding **ed** to a word means it happened in the past.

Directions: Look at the words in the word box. Underline the root word in each one. Write a word to complete each sentence.

snowing	wished	played	looking	crying
talking	walked	eating	going	doing

1. We like to play. We _____ yesterday.

2. Is that snow? Yes, it is _____.

3. Do you want to go with me? No, I am _____ with my friend.

4. The baby will cry if we leave. The baby is _____.

5. We will walk home from school. We _____ to school this morning.

6. Did you wish for a new bike? Yes, I _____ for one.

7. Who is going to do it while we are away? I am

   _____ it.

8. Did you talk to your friend? Yes, we are

   _____ now.

9. Will you look at my book? I am _____ at it now.

10. I like to eat pizza. We are _____ it today.

Directions: Write a word from the word box next to its root word.

coming	running	sitting	lived	rained
swimming	visited	carried	racing	hurried

run _____ come _____

live _____ carry _____

hurry _____ race _____

swim _____ rain _____

visit _____ sit _____

Directions: Write a word from the word box to finish each sentence.

1. I _____ my grandmother during vacation.

2. Mary went _____ at the lake with her cousin.

3. Jim _____ the heavy package for his mother.

4. It _____ and stormed all weekend.

5. Cars go very fast when they are _____ .

Suffixes

Directions: Add one of the endings in the box to each root word. Write the correct form of the word to finish each sentence.

ed	ing

1. When my dog was a puppy, he often _____ on old shoes and slippers. **chew**

2. When we saw the cat, it was _____ a tree. **climb**

3. We _____ the street to catch the bus. **cross**

4. Mike was _____ in the rain. **walk**

5. A tiny baby is usually either _____ or sleeping. **eat**

6. I _____ David to show me his kitten. **ask**

7. The children were _____ ball in the yard. **play**

8. A big dog _____ at us when we walked by. **bark**

9. I _____ a fish with my fishing pole. **hook**

Suffixes

Word families have the same root word in common.

Example: play
plays
played
playing

Directions: Add **s**, **ed**, and **ing** to each root word to create word families.

work	talk	bark
_____	_____	_____
_____	_____	_____
_____	_____	_____

walk	cook	jump
_____	_____	_____
_____	_____	_____
_____	_____	_____

Suffixes

A **suffix** is a syllable that is added at the end of a word to change its meaning.

Directions: Add the suffixes to the root word to make new words. Then, use your new words to complete the sentences.

help + ful = _____

care + less = _____

build + er = _____

talk + ed = _____

love + ly = _____

loud + er = _____

1. My mother _____ to my teacher about my homework.

2. The radio was _____ than the television.

3. Sally is always _____ to her mother.

4. A _____ put a new garage on our house.

5. The flowers are _____ .

6. It is _____ to cross the street without looking both ways.

Directions: Read the story. Underline the words that end with **est**, **ed**, or **ing**. On the lines below, write the root words for each word you underlined.

The funniest book I ever read was about a girl named Nan. Nan did everything backward. She even spelled her name backward. Nan slept in the day and played at night. She dried her hair before washing it. She turned on the light after she finished her book—which she read from the back to the front!
When it rained, Nan waited until she was inside before opening her umbrella. She even walked backward. The silliest part: The only thing Nan did forward was back up!

1. _____

2. _____

3. _____

4. _____

5. _____

6. _____

7. _____

8. _____

9. _____

10. _____

11. _____

12. _____

13. _____

94

Review

Directions: Read the word in bold in each sentence and circle each suffix. Write the root word on the line. Remember, some root words are changed when an ending is added.

Example: silliness ➤ silly

1. Sue and Tim were **dancing** at the party. _____

2. The children were **careful** not to play in the street. _____

3. We made a mistake and put the door on **backward**. _____

4. This is the **funniest** movie I ever saw. _____

5. A new baby is **helpless**. _____

6. I **asked** Mike to bring his wagon to my house. _____

7. I'm really tired today because I had a **sleepless** night. _____

8. My teacher is **really** nice. _____

9. The book I am **reading** is good. _____

10. Everyone wants to find **happiness**. _____

11. The game isn't **likely** to end soon. _____

12. My plant seems to grow **taller** every day. _____

Directions: Read the prefix and its meaning. Add each prefix to a root word to make a new word. Write the new word. Then, finish the sentences using the words you just wrote.

Prefixes	(Meaning)	Root Word	New Word
bi	(two)	cycle	_____
dis	(away from)	appear	_____
ex	(out of)	change	_____
im	(not)	polite	_____
in	(within)	side	_____
mis	(wrong)	place	_____
non	(not)	sense	_____
pre	(before)	school	_____
re	(again)	build	_____
un	(not)	happy	_____

1. Did you go to _____ before kindergarten?

2. The magician made the rabbit _____ .

3. Put your things where they belong so you don't

   _____ them.

4. Can you ride a _____ ?

5. Do you want to _____ your shirt for one that fits?

Prefixes

Directions: Read the story. Change Unlucky Sam to Lucky Sam by taking the **un** prefix off of the **bold** words.

Unlucky Sam

Sam was **unhappy** about a lot of things in his life. His parents were **uncaring**. His teacher was **unfair**. His big sister was **unkind**. His neighbors were **unfriendly**. He was **unhealthy**, too! How could one boy be as **unlucky** as Sam?

Lucky Sam

Sam was _____ about a lot of things in his

life. His parents were _____ . His teacher was

_____ . His big sister was _____ .

His neighbors were _____. He was

_____ , too! How could one boy be as

_____ as Sam?

Directions: Change the meaning of the sentences by adding the prefixes to the **bold** words.

The boy was **lucky** because he guessed the answer **correctly**.

The boy was (un) _____ because he guessed the

answer (in) _____ .

When Mary **behaved**, she felt **happy**.

When Mary (mis) _____ ,

she felt (un) _____ .

Mike wore his jacket **buttoned** because the dance was **formal**.

Mike wore his jacket (un) _____ because the

dance was (in) _____.

Tim **understood** because he was **familiar** with the book.

Tim (mis) _____ because he was

(un) _____ with the book.

Directions: Read the story. Change the story by removing the prefix **re** from the **bold** words. Write the new words in the new story.

Repete is a **rewriter** who has to **redo** every story. He has to **rethink** up the ideas. He has to **rewrite** the sentences. He has to **redraw** the pictures. He even has to **retype** the pages. Who will **repay Repete** for all the work he **redoes**?

_____ is a _____ who has to

_____ every story. He has to _____

up the ideas. He has to _____ the sentences.

He has to _____ the pictures. He even has to

_____ the pages. Who will _____

_____ for all the work he _____ ?

Prefixes and Suffixes

Directions: See how many new words you can make by adding prefixes and suffixes to the root words. You can use the prefixes, suffixes, and root words as many times as you like.

Prefixes:

bi   dis   ex   in   im   mis   non   pre   re   un

Root Words:

play   obey   friend   feel   health
polite   kind   thought   cycle   like

Suffixes:

ly   ing   ed   y   ful   ness   less   able   ment

_____

_____

_____

_____

_____

Prefixes and Suffixes

Directions: See how many words you can find. The words can go up, down, left, right, or diagonal.

unhappy	tricycle	disappoint
excite	impress	misfit
preschool	unsafe	friendly
singing	played	sleepy
likeable	kindness	

```
d  i  s  a  p  p  o  i  n  t  n  p
a  b  e  f  l  r  m  s  o  a  c  l
w  y  v  r  e  e  u  s  k  e  n  a
f  h  r  m  s  s  l  e  e  p  y  y
r  p  u  i  u  c  t  n  t  z  x  e
i  n  m  s  a  h  r  d  i  s  l  d
e  g  i  f  v  o  i  n  w  s  g  i
n  y  y  i  z  o  c  i  p  e  c  h
d  c  n  t  m  l  y  k  g  r  e  r
l  i  k  u  l  p  c  i  o  p  q  n
y  d  v  h  p  d  l  t  j  m  i  f
j  v  l  a  f  p  e  x  c  i  t  e
d  s  h  l  i  k  e  a  b  l  e  p
r  n  n  g  k  g  n  i  g  n  i  s
u  n  s  a  f  e  s  b  k  t  o  m
```

Directions: Read each sentence. Look at the words in **bold**. Circle the prefix and write the root word on the line.

1. The **preview** of the movie was funny. _____

2. We always drink **nonfat** milk. _____

3. We will have to **reschedule** the trip. _____

4. Are you tired of **reruns** on television? _____

5. I have **outgrown** my new shoes already. _____

6. You must have **misplaced** the papers. _____

7. Police **enforce** the laws of the city. _____

8. I **disliked** that book. _____

9. The boy **distrusted** the big dog. _____

10. Try to **enjoy** yourself at the party. _____

11. Please try to keep the cat **inside** the house. _____

12. That song is total **nonsense**! _____

13. We will **replace** any parts that we lost. _____

14. Can you help me **unzip** this jacket? _____

15. Let's **rework** today's arithmetic problems. _____

Create-a-Word

Directions: Create words by using letters that are connected. See how many you can make!

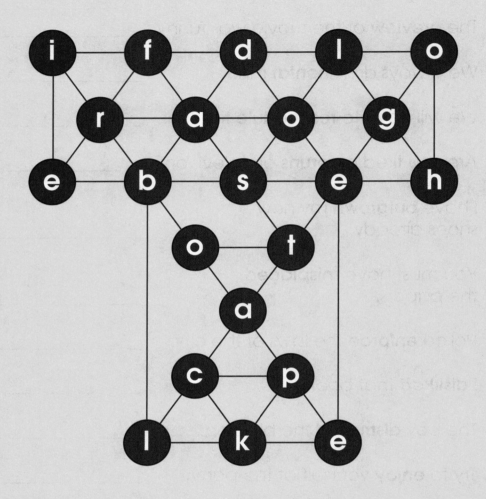

_____   _____   _____

_____   _____   _____

_____   _____   _____

_____   _____   _____

_____   _____   _____

Parts of a Story

Characters are the people or animals in a story.

Directions: Match the familiar stories with the correct characters.

"The Three Bears" •   • Giant

"Peter Cottontail" •   • Goldilocks

"The Three Little Pigs" •   • Fairy Godmother

"Little Red Riding Hood" •   • Granny

"Jack and the Beanstalk" •   • The Wolf

"Cinderella" •   • Flopsy and Mopsy

Think of some of your favorite stories. What other characters do you know? Write them.

_____

_____

_____

_____

Parts of a Book

A book has many parts. The **title** is the name of the book. The **author** is the person who wrote the words. The **illustrator** is the person who drew the pictures. The **table of contents** is located at the beginning to list what is in the book. The **glossary** is a little dictionary in the back to help you with unfamiliar words. Books are often divided into smaller sections of information called **chapters**.

Directions: Look at one of your books. Write the parts you see below.

The title of my book is _____

The author is _____

The illustrator is _____

My book has a table of contents.   Yes or No

My book has a glossary.   Yes or No

My book is divided into chapters.   Yes or No

Here is a recipe for chocolate peanut butter cookies. When you use a recipe, you must follow the directions carefully. The sentences below are not in the correct order.

Directions: Write **1** to show what you would do first. Then, number each step to show the correct sequence.

_____ Melt the chocolate almond bark in a microsafe bowl.

_____ Eat!

_____ While the chocolate is melting, spread peanut butter on a cracker and place another cracker on top.

_____ Let the melted candy drip off the cracker into the bowl before you place it on wax paper.

_____ Let it cool!

_____ Carefully use a fork or spoon to dip the crackers into the melted chocolate.

Try the recipe with an adult.

Do you like to cook? _____

Glossary

Alphabetical (ABC) Order: Putting letters or words in the order in which they appear in the alphabet.

Antonyms: Words that mean the opposite. **Examples: big** and **small**.

Author: The person who wrote the words of a book.

Chapters: Small sections of a book.

Characters: The people or animals in a story.

Classifying: Putting similar things into groups.

Compound Words: Two words that are put together to make one new word.

Consonant Blends: Two or three consonant letters in a word whose sounds combine, or blend. **Examples: br, fr, gr, tr.**

Consonant Teams: Two or three consonant letters that have the single sound. **Examples: sh** and **tch**.

Double Vowel Words: When two vowels appear together in a word. **Examples:** t**ea**, c**oa**t.

Glossary: A little dictionary at the back of a book.

Hard and Soft c: In words where **c** is followed by **a** or **u**, the **c** usually has the hard sound (like a **k**). **Examples: c**up, **c**art. When **c** is followed by **e, i,** or **y**, it usually has a soft sound (like an **s**). **Examples: circle, fence.**

Hard and Soft g: When **g** is followed by **e, i,** or **y**, it usually has a soft sound (like **j**). **Examples:** chan**g**e and **g**entle. The hard **g** sounds like the **g** in **g**irl or **g**ate.

Illustrator: The person who drew pictures for a book.

Long Vowels: Long vowels say their names. **Examples: Long a** is the sound you hear in h**a**y. **Long e** is the sound you hear in m**e**. **Long i** is the sound you hear in p**i**e. **Long o** is the sound you hear in n**o**. **Long u** is the sound you hear in c**u**te.

Ordinal Numbers: Number words telling order. **Example: first**.

Glossary

Plurals: Words that mean more than one. **Examples: shoes, ladies, dishes, foxes**.

Prefix: A syllable added at the beginning of a word to change its meaning. **Examples: dis**appear, **mis**place.

R-Controlled Vowel: When **r** follows a vowel, it gives the vowel a different sound. **Examples:** h**er**, b**ar**k, b**ir**d.

Short Vowels: Vowels that make short sounds. **Examples: Short a** is the sound you hear in c**a**t. **Short e** is the sound you hear in l**e**g. **Short i** is the sound you hear in p**i**g. **Short o** is the sound in b**o**x. **Short u** is the sound in c**u**p.

Silent Letters: Letters you can't hear at all. **Examples:** the **gh** in ni**gh**t, the **w** in **w**rong, and the **t** in lis**t**en.

Simile: A figure of speech that compares two things that are alike in some way. The words **like** and **as** are used in similes. **Examples: as soft as a pillow, as light as a feather**.

Suffix: a syllable added at the end of a word to change its meaning. **Examples:** small**er**, help**less**.

Super Silent e: An **e** that you can't hear when it appears at the end of a word. It makes the other vowel have a long sound. **Examples:** cap**e**, rob**e**, slid**e**.

Syllables: The parts of words that have vowel sounds. **Examples: Rab bit** has two syllables. **Bas ket ball** has three syllables.

Synonyms: Words that mean the same or nearly the same. **Examples: sleepy** and **tired**.

Table of Contents: A list at the beginning of a book, telling what is in the book by page number.

Title: The name of a book.

Vowel Team: Vowels that appear together in words. Usually, the first one says its name and the second one is silent. **Examples:** le**a**f, s**oa**p, r**ai**n.

Y as a Vowel: When **y** comes at the end of a word, it is a vowel. **Examples:** m**y**, bab**y**.

3 — Zoo Animal Riddles

Directions: Write the name of the animal that answers each riddle.

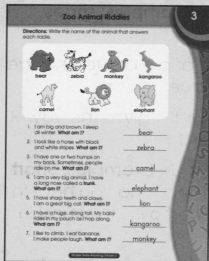

bear zebra monkey kangaroo
camel lion elephant

1. I am big and brown. I sleep all winter. **What am I?** — bear
2. I look like a horse with black and white stripes. **What am I?** — zebra
3. I have one or two humps on my back. Sometimes, people ride on me. **What am I?** — camel
4. I am a very big animal. I have a long nose called a **trunk**. **What am I?** — elephant
5. I have sharp teeth and claws. I am a great big cat. **What am I?** — lion
6. I have a huge, strong tail. My baby rides in my pouch as I hop along. **What am I?** — kangaroo
7. I like to climb. I eat bananas. I make people laugh. **What am I?** — monkey

3

4 — Help the Animals Find Their Cages

Directions: The animals have escaped from their cages! The zookeeper needs your help to get them back where they belong. Draw a line from the animal to the cage with its name on it.

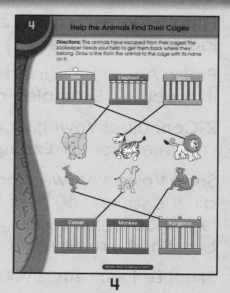

4

5 — Zoo Animals Word Find

Directions: All the words below are things you might see in a zoo. Find the zoo words hidden in the puzzle. The words can be up, down, or across. Look at the examples.

monkey	tiger	ape
zoo	keeper	cage
snake	giraffe	ostrich
seal	shark	peacock
elephant	bear	zebra
food	emu	moose
lion	fish	bat

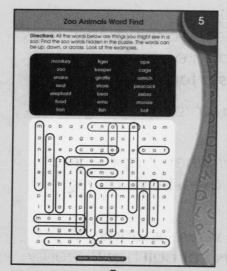

5

6 — Reading for Details

Directions: Draw a line from the sign to the sentence that tells about it.

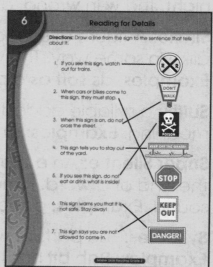

1. If you see this sign, watch out for trains.
2. When cars or bikes come to this sign, they must stop.
3. When this sign is on, do not cross the street.
4. This sign tells you to stay out of the yard.
5. If you see this sign, do not eat or drink what is inside!
6. This sign warns you that it is not safe. Stay away!
7. This sign says you are not allowed to come in.

6

7 — Reading for Details

Directions: Read the story about bike safety. Answer the questions below the story.

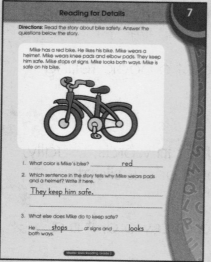

Mike has a red bike. He likes his bike. Mike wears a helmet. Mike wears knee pads and elbow pads. They keep him safe. Mike stops at signs. Mike looks both ways. Mike is safe on his bike.

1. What color is Mike's bike? — red
2. Which sentence in the story tells why Mike wears pads and a helmet? Write it here. — They keep him safe.
3. What else does Mike do to keep safe? — He stops at signs and looks both ways.

7

8 — Ordinal Numbers

Directions: Look at the **ordinal words** in the box. Write each word on the correct line to put the words in order.

second	fifth	seventh	first	tenth
third	eighth	sixth	fourth	ninth

1. first
2. second
3. third
4. fourth
5. fifth
6. sixth
7. seventh
8. eighth
9. ninth
10. tenth

Directions: Which picture is circled in each row? Underline the correct ordinal word.

- third — **fourth**
- fourth — **sixth**
- first — **ninth**
- **third** — fifth
- fifth — **sixth**
- **second** — third
- ninth — **tenth**
- **first** — second

8

9 — Ordinal Numbers

Directions: Look at the pictures. Write the correct ordinal word.

first	second	third	fourth	fifth
sixth	seventh	eighth	ninth	tenth

- fifth
- second
- sixth
- first
- fourth
- sixth
- ninth
- tenth

Master Skills Reading Grade 2

9

10 — Reading for Details

Directions: Read the story about baby animals. Answer the questions with words from the story.

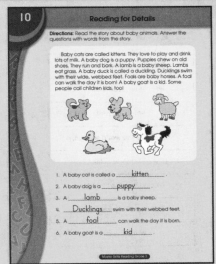

Baby cats are called kittens. They love to play and drink lots of milk. A baby dog is a puppy. Puppies chew on old shoes. They run and bark. A lamb is a baby sheep. Lambs eat grass. A baby duck is called a duckling. Ducklings swim with their wide, webbed feet. Foals are baby horses. A foal can walk the day it is born! A baby goat is a kid. Some people call children kids, too!

1. A baby cat is called a __kitten__
2. A baby dog is a __puppy__
3. A __lamb__ is a baby sheep.
4. __Ducklings__ swim with their webbed feet.
5. A __foal__ can walk the day it is born.
6. A baby goat is a __kid__

Master Skills Reading Grade 2

10

11 — Reading for Details

Directions: Read the story about different kinds of transportation. Answer the questions with words from the story.

People use many kinds of transportation. Boats float on the water. Some people fish in a boat. Airplanes fly in the sky. Flying in a plane is a fast way to get somewhere. Trains run on a track. The first car is the engine. The last car is the caboose. Some people even sleep in beds on a train! A car has four wheels. Most people have a car. A car rides on roads. A bus can hold many people. A bus rides on roads. Most children ride a bus to school.

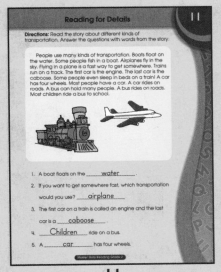

1. A boat floats on the __water__.
2. If you want to get somewhere fast, which transportation would you use? __airplane__
3. The first car on a train is called an engine and the last car is a __caboose__
4. __Children__ ride on a bus.
5. A __car__ has four wheels.

Master Skills Reading Grade 2

11

12 — Riddle

Directions: Use the key to match the number with the letter. Write the riddle and the answer.

WHAT DID THE
4 19 26 7 19 22

LETTER SAY TO
15 22 7 7 22 9 8 26 2 7 12

THE STAMP?
7 19 22 8 7 26 14 11

Answer:

STICK TO ME
8 7 18 24 16 7 12 14 22

AND WE WILL
26 13 23 4 22 4 18 15 15

GO PLACES.
20 12 11 15 26 24 22 8

Key:

A	B	C	D	E	F	G	H	I	J	K	L	M
26	25	24	23	22	21	20	19	18	17	16	15	14

N	O	P	Q	R	S	T	U	V	W	X	Y	Z
13	12	11	10	9	8	7	6	5	4	3	2	1

Master Skills Reading Grade 2

12

13 — Nursery Rhyme Riddles

Directions: Write the name of the character to answer the riddle.

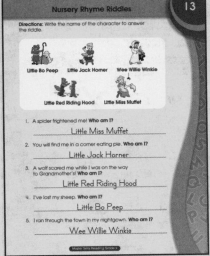

Little Bo Peep   Little Jack Horner   Wee Willie Winkie

Little Red Riding Hood   Little Miss Muffet

1. A spider frightened me! **Who am I?**
   __Little Miss Muffet__
2. You will find me in a corner eating pie. **Who am I?**
   __Little Jack Horner__
3. A wolf scared me while I was on the way to Grandmother's! **Who am I?**
   __Little Red Riding Hood__
4. I've lost my sheep. **Who am I?**
   __Little Bo Peep__
5. I ran through the town in my nightgown. **Who am I?**
   __Wee Willie Winkie__

Master Skills Reading Grade 2

13

14 — Nursery Rhyme Jumble

Directions: The nursery rhymes are all mixed up! Draw lines to show what the next line should be.

Hint: If you don't know them all, look for rhymes.

Baa, baa, black sheep,   —   come again another day.

One, two, buckle my shoe.   —   sat on a tuffet.

Hickory, dickory, dock.   —   three men in a tub.

Hey, diddle, diddle,   —   How I wonder what you are!

Jack and Jill went up the hill   —   the cat and the fiddle.

Rub-a-dub-dub,   —   to fetch a pail of water.

Twinkle, twinkle, little star,   —   have you any wool?

Rain, rain go away,   —   The mouse ran up the clock.

Little Miss Muffet   —   has lost her sheep.

Little Bo Peep   —   Three, four, shut the door.

Master Skills Reading Grade 2

14

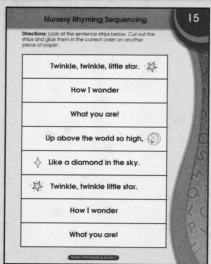

Nursery Rhyming Sequencing — 15

Directions: Look at the sentence strips below. Cut out the strips and glue them in the correct order on another piece of paper.

- Twinkle, twinkle, little star.
- How I wonder
- What you are!
- Up above the world so high,
- Like a diamond in the sky.
- Twinkle, twinkle little star.
- How I wonder
- What you are!

15

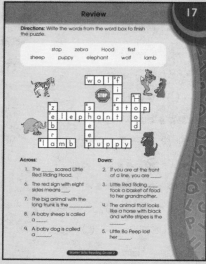

Review — 17

Directions: Write the words from the word box to finish the puzzle.

stop   zebra   Hood   first
sheep   puppy   elephant   wolf   lamb

Across:
1. The _____ scared Little Red Riding Hood.
6. The red sign with eight sides means ___.
7. The big animal with the long trunk is the _____.
8. A baby sheep is called a ____.
9. A baby dog is called a ____.

Down:
2. If you are at the front of a line, you are ____.
3. Little Red Riding ____ took a basket of food to her grandmother.
4. The animal that looks like a horse with black and white stripes is the ____.
5. Little Bo Peep lost her ____.

17

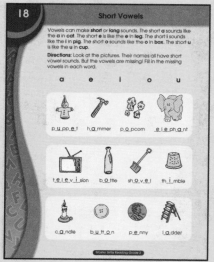

Short Vowels — 18

Vowels can make **short** or **long** sounds. The short **a** sounds like the **a** in **cat**. The short **e** is like the **e** in **leg**. The short **i** sounds like the **i** in **pig**. The short **o** sounds like the **o** in **box**. The short **u** is like the **u** in **cup**.

Directions: Look at the pictures. Their names all have short vowel sounds. But the vowels are missing! Fill in the missing vowels in each word.

a   e   i   o   u

p u pp e t   h a mmer   p o pcorn   e l e ph a nt

t e l e v i sion   b o ttle   sh o vel   th i mble

c a ndle   b u tt o n   p e nny   l a dder

18

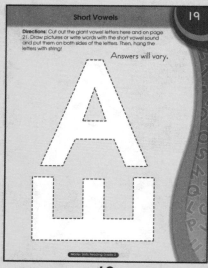

Short Vowels — 19

Directions: Cut out the giant vowel letters here and on page 21. Draw pictures or write words with the short vowel sound and put them on both sides of the letters. Then, hang the letters with string!

Answers will vary.

A
E

19

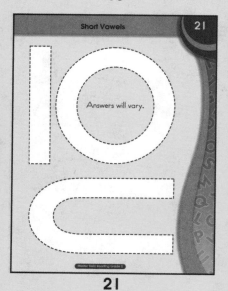

Short Vowels — 21

Answers will vary.

I
O
U

21

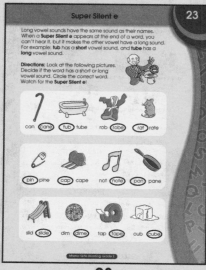

Super Silent e — 23

Long vowel sounds have the same sound as their names. When a **Super Silent e** appears at the end of a word, you can't hear it, but it makes the other vowel have a long sound. For example: **tub** has a **short** vowel sound, and **tube** has a **long** vowel sound.

Directions: Look at the following pictures. Decide if the word has a short or long vowel sound. Circle the correct word. Watch for the **Super Silent e**!

can (cane)   tub (tube)   rob (robe)   rat (rate)

pin (pine)   cap (cape)   not (note)   pan (pane)

slid (slide)   dim (dime)   tap (tape)   cub (cube)

23

24 — Double Vowel Words

Usually when two vowels appear together, the first one says its name and the second one is silent.
Example: bean

Directions: Unscramble the double vowel words below. Write the correct word on the line.

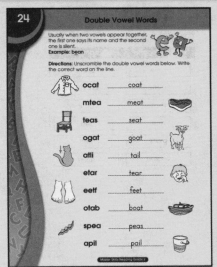

- ocat — coat
- mtea — meat
- teas — seat
- ogat — goat
- atli — tail
- etar — tear
- eetf — feet
- otab — boat
- spea — peas
- apli — pail

Master Skills Reading Grade 2

24

25 — Long Vowels

Directions: Read the paragraph. Write the words with the long vowel sounds (**remember:** long vowels say their names) on the lines where they belong. (If a word appears more than once, don't write it again.)

In winter, Jake, Pete, and Bruce like to skate. They go to the lake at the park with other boys and girls. There is one important rule: You must make sure the lake is frozen. Do not skate if the sign reads "ICE NOT SAFE." The park ranger builds a fire for the children to warm their hands. The smoke circles over the pine and spruce trees.

Words with Long a			
J a k e	s kat e	l ak e	m ak e	s af e

Words with Long e			
P et e	t ree s		

Words with Long i			
l ik e	s ign	ice	f ire	p ine

Words with Long o			
g o	fr oze n	s moke	ov er

Words with Long u			
B ruc e	r ul e	sp ruce	

Master Skills Reading Grade 2

25

26 — R-Controlled Vowels

When a vowel is followed by the letter **r**, it has a different sound.
Example: he and her

Directions: Write a word from the word box to finish each sentence. Notice the sound of the vowel followed by an **r**.

park	chair	horse	bark	bird
hurt	girl	hair	store	ears

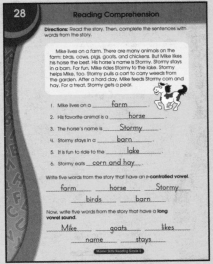

1. A dog likes to ___bark___.
2. You buy food at a ___store___.
3. Children like to play at the ___park___.
4. An animal you can ride is a ___horse___.
5. You hear with your ___ears___.
6. A robin is a kind of ___bird___.
7. If you fall down, you might get ___hurt___.
8. The opposite of a boy is a ___girl___.
9. You comb and brush your ___hair___.
10. You sit down on a ___chair___.

Master Skills Reading Grade 2

26

27 — R-Controlled Vowels

Directions: Answer the riddles below. You will need to complete the words with the correct vowel followed by r.

1. I am something you may use to eat. **What am I?**

   f ___or___ k

2. My word names the opposite of tall. **What am I?**

   sh ___or___ t

3. I can be seen high in the sky. I twinkle. **What am I?**

   st ___ar___

4. I am a kind of clothing a girl might wear. **What am I?**

   sk ___ir___ t

5. My word tells what a group of cows is called. **What am I?**

   h ___er___ d

6. I am part of your body. **What am I?**

   ___ar___ m

Master Skills Reading Grade 2

27

28 — Reading Comprehension

Directions: Read the story. Then, complete the sentences with words from the story.

Mike lives on a farm. There are many animals on the farm: birds, cows, pigs, goats, and chickens. But Mike likes his horse the best. His horse's name is Stormy. Stormy stays in a barn. For fun, Mike rides Stormy to the lake. Stormy helps Mike, too. Stormy pulls a cart to carry weeds from the garden. After a hard day, Mike feeds Stormy corn and hay. For a treat, Stormy gets a pear.

1. Mike lives on a ___farm___.
2. His favorite animal is a ___horse___.
3. The horse's name is ___Stormy___.
4. Stormy stays in a ___barn___.
5. It is fun to ride to the ___lake___.
6. Stormy eats ___corn and hay___.

Write five words from the story that have an **r-controlled vowel.**

___farm___   ___horse___   ___Stormy___
___birds___   ___barn___

Now, write five words from the story that have a **long vowel sound.**

___Mike___   ___goats___   ___likes___
___name___   ___stays___

Master Skills Reading Grade 2

28

29 — Hard and Soft c

When c is followed by **e, i,** or **y,** it usually has a **soft** sound. The **soft c** sounds like **s. Example:** circle and fence. When c is followed by **a, o** or **u,** it usually has a **hard** sound. The **hard c** sounds like **k. Example:** cup and cart.

Directions: Read the words in the word box. Write the words in the correct lists. Then, write a word from the word box to finish each sentence. The first one is done for you.

pencil	cookie	dance	cent	popcorn
circus	lucky	mice	tractor	card

Words with soft c	Words with hard c
pencil	popcorn
dance	lucky
cent	tractor
mice	cookie
circus	card

1. Another word for a penny is a ___cent___.
2. A cat likes to chase ___mice___.
3. You will see animals and clowns at the ___circus___.
4. We like to ___dance___ to the music.
5. Will you please sharpen my ___pencil___?

Master Skills Reading Grade 2

29

Answer Key

30 — Hard and Soft g

When **g** is followed by **e**, **i**, or **y**, it usually has a **soft** sound. The **soft g** sounds like **j**. **Example:** change and gentle. The **hard g** sounds like the **g** in girl or gate.

Directions: Read the words in the word box. Write the words in the correct lists. Then, write a word from the box to finish each sentence. The first one is done for you.

engine	glove	cage	magic	frog
giant	flag	large	glass	goose

Words with soft g	Words with hard g
engine	glove
giant	flag
cage	glass
large	frog
magic	goose

1. Our bird lives in a __cage__.
2. Pulling a rabbit from a hat is a good __magic__ trick.
3. A car needs an __engine__ to run.
4. A __giant__ is a huge person.
5. An elephant is a very __large__ animal.

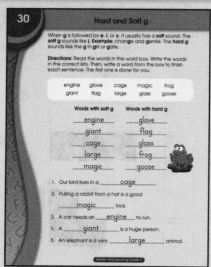

30

31 — Hard and Soft c and g

Directions: Look at the c and g words at the bottom of the page. Cut them out and glue them in the correct box below.

🗑 soft sound	✂ hard sound
juice	grass
gem	crayon
face	goat
age	jug
giant	cart
engine	grow

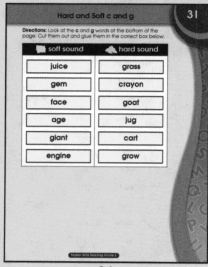

31

33 — Y as a Vowel

When **y** comes at the end of a word, it is a vowel. When **y** is the only vowel at the end of a one-syllable word, it has the sound of a long **i** (like in **my**). When **y** is the only vowel at the end of a word with more than one syllable, it has the sound of a long **e** (like in **baby**).

Directions: Look at the words in the word box. If the word has the sound of a long **i**, write it under the word **my**. If the word has the sound of a long **e**, write it under the word **baby**. Then, write the word from the word box that answers each riddle.

happy	penny	fry	try	sleepy	dry
bunny	why	windy	sky	party	fly

my	baby
why	happy
fry	bunny
try	penny
sky	windy
dry	sleepy
fly	party

1. It takes five of these to make a nickel. __penny__
2. This is what you call a baby rabbit. __bunny__
3. It is often blue and you can see it if you look up. __sky__
4. You might have one of these on your birthday. __party__
5. It is the opposite of wet. __dry__

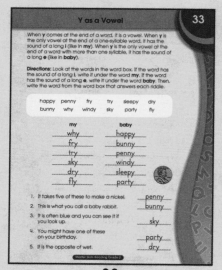

33

34 — Vowel Teams

Usually when two vowels appear together, the first one says its name and the second one is silent.

Directions: Find the words in the puzzle. Then, write words from the word box to finish the sentences.

meal	soap	sea	loaf	tail
toe	rain	leaves	coat	toast

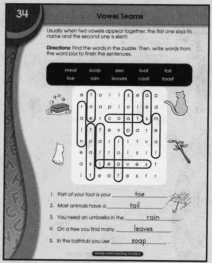

1. Part of your foot is your __toe__.
2. Most animals have a __tail__.
3. You need an umbrella in the __rain__.
4. On a tree you find many __leaves__.
5. In the bathtub you use __soap__.

34

35 — Vowel Teams

The vowel teams **ou** and **ow** can have the same sound. You can hear it in the words **clown** and **cloud**. The vowel teams **au** and **aw** have the same sound. You hear it in the words **because** and **law**.

Directions: Look at the pictures. Write the correct vowel team to complete the words. You may need to use a dictionary to help you with the correct spelling. The first one is done for you.

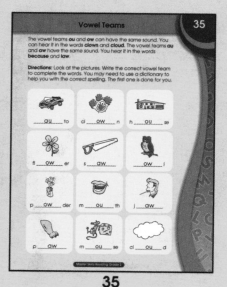

__au__to cl__ow__n h__ou__se

fl__ow__er s__aw__ __ow__l

p__ow__der m__ou__th j__aw__

p__aw__ m__ou__se cl__ou__d

35

36 — Vowel Teams

The vowel teams **oi** and **oy** have the same sound. You can hear it in the words **oil** and **boy**.

Directions: Finish the sentences by writing the correct word from the word box.

boil	point	coin	boy	toy
joy	join	enjoy	voice	soil

1. You need a pencil with a sharp __point__.
2. A dime is a kind of __coin__.
3. Leah's doll is her favorite __toy__.
4. The opposite of girl is __boy__.
5. To be a member of a club you must __join__.
6. Another word for dirt is __soil__.
7. When you talk, we hear your __voice__.
8. Ice cream is a dessert I __enjoy__.
9. If water is very hot, it will __boil__.
10. Another word for happiness is __joy__.

36

37 — Vowel Teams

The vowel team **oo** has two sounds. You can remember them with this sentence: Your **foot** goes in your **boot**.

Directions: Look at the pictures. Say their names. If the vowel sounds like the **oo** in **foot**, draw a line to the foot. If it sounds like the **oo** in **boot**, draw a line to the boot.

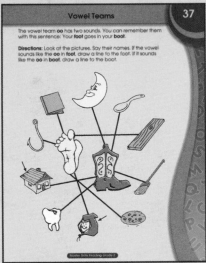

Master Skills Reading Grade 2

37

38 — Vowel Teams

The vowel team **ea** can have a short **e** sound like in **head**, or a long **e** sound like in **bead**. An **ea** followed by an **r** makes a sound like the one in **ear** or like the one in **heard**.

Directions: Read the story. Listen for the sound **ea** makes in the bold words.

Have you ever **read** a book or **heard** a story about a **bear**? You might have **learned** that bears sleep through the winter. Some bears may sleep the whole **season**. Sometimes, they look almost **dead**. But they are very much alive. As the cold winter passes and the spring **weather** comes **near**, they wake up. After such a nice rest, they must be **ready** to **eat** a **really** big **meal**!

words with long ea	words with short ea	ea followed by r
season	read	heard
eat	dead	bear
really	weather	learned
meal	ready	near

Master Skills Reading Grade 2

38

39 — Vowel Teams

The vowel team **ie** makes the long **e** sound like in **believe**. The team **ei** also makes the long **e** sound like in **either**. But **ei** can also make a long **a** sound like in **eight**.

Directions: Circle the **ei** words with the long **a** sound.

(neighbor)   (veil)

receive   (reindeer)

(reign)   ceiling

The teams **eigh** and **ey** also make the long **a** sound.

Directions: Finish the sentences with words from the word box.

chief   sleigh   obey   weigh   thief   field   ceiling

1. Eight reindeer pull Santa's ___sleigh___ .
2. Rules are for us to ___obey___ .
3. The bird got out of its cage and flew up to the ___ceiling___ .
4. The leader of an Indian tribe is the ___chief___ .
5. How much do you ___weigh___ ?
6. They caught the ___thief___ who took my bike.
7. Corn grows in a ___field___ .

Master Skills Reading Grade 2

39

40 — Vowel Team Scramble

Directions: Unscramble the letters to create words. Draw a picture next to each word.

eamt	meat
toab	boat
sial	sail
mseou	mouse
cnoi	coin
oyt	toy
tobo	boot
koob	book
brdea	bread
leiv	veil or live

Drawings will vary.

Master Skills Reading Grade 2

40

41 — Review

Directions: Read the story. Fill in the blanks with words from the word box.

cookies   Joe   bowl   tooth   flour   eight
spoon   eats   enjoys   round   boy   either

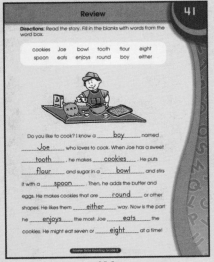

Do you like to cook? I know a ___boy___ named ___Joe___ who loves to cook. When Joe has a sweet ___tooth___ , he makes ___cookies___ . He puts ___flour___ and sugar in a ___bowl___ and stirs it with a ___spoon___ . Then, he adds the butter and eggs. He makes cookies that are ___round___ or other shapes. He likes them ___either___ way. Now is the part he ___enjoys___ the most: Joe ___eats___ the cookies. He might eat seven or ___eight___ at a time!

Master Skills Reading Grade 2

41

42 — School Words

Directions: Fill in the blanks with a word from the word box.

pencil   teacher   crayons
recess   lunchbox   play
fun   math

1. I need to sharpen my ___pencil___ .
2. I like to ___play___ at recess.
3. School is ___fun___ !
4. My ___teacher___ helps me learn.
5. I need to color the picture with ___crayons___ .
6. I play kickball at ___recess___ .
7. My sandwich is in my ___lunchbox___ .
8. In ___math___ I can add and subtract.

Master Skills Reading Grade 2

42

43 — Money Words

Directions: Fill in the blanks with a word from the word box.

penny	nickel	dime
quarter	dollar	cent
check	bank	savings

1. Some people call one cent a "lucky ___penny___."
2. Mom can write a ___check___ to buy things.
3. I put some money in my ___savings (bank)___ account.
4. Ten cents or a ___dime___ is equal to 10 pennies.
5. One ___cent___ is a penny.
6. I have 100¢ or one ___dollar___.
7. I bought some gum with 25¢ or a ___quarter___.
8. Five cents is also known as a ___nickel___.
9. Make your own sentence using the leftover word.

___Answers will vary.___

43

44 — Days of the Week

Directions: Write the day of the week that answers each question.

Sunday	Monday	Tuesday
Wednesday	Thursday	Friday
Saturday		

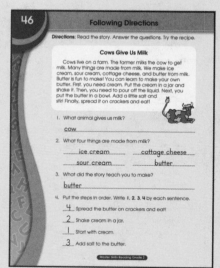

1. What is the first day of the week?
___Sunday___
2. What is the last day of the week?
___Saturday___
3. What day comes after Tuesday?
___Wednesday___
4. What day comes between Wednesday and Friday?
___Thursday___
5. What is the third day of the week?
___Tuesday___
6. What day comes before Saturday?
___Friday___
7. What day comes after Sunday?
___Monday___

44

45 — Months of the Year

Directions: Write the name of the month that answers each question.

January	February	March	April
May	June	July	August
September	October	November	December

1. Spring starts in the third month. **What is it?**
___March___
2. In some places, school starts the month after August. **What is it?**
___September___
3. Christmas is in the last month of the year. **What is it?**
___December___
4. Summer starts in the sixth month. **What is it?**
___June___
5. Columbus Day is in the month before November. **What is it?**
___October___
6. The second month has the fewest days. **What is it?**
___February___
7. This is the first month of the year. **What is it?**
___January___

45

46 — Following Directions

Directions: Read the story. Answer the questions. Try the recipe.

Cows Give Us Milk

Cows live on a farm. The farmer milks the cow to get milk. Many things are made from milk. We make ice cream, sour cream, cottage cheese, and butter from milk. Butter is fun to make! You can learn to make your own butter. First, you need cream. Put the cream in a jar and shake it. Then, you need to pour off the liquid. Next, you put the butter in a bowl. Add a little salt and stir. Finally, spread it on crackers and eat!

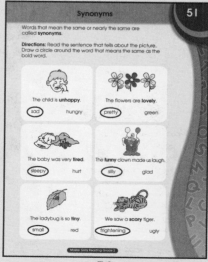

1. What animal gives us milk?
cow
2. What four things are made from milk?
___ice cream___ ___cottage cheese___
___sour cream___ ___butter___
3. What did the story teach you to make?
butter
4. Put the steps in order. Write **1, 2, 3, 4** by each sentence.
___4___ Spread the butter on crackers and eat!
___2___ Shake cream in a jar.
___1___ Start with cream.
___3___ Add salt to the butter.

46

49 — Silly Sentences!

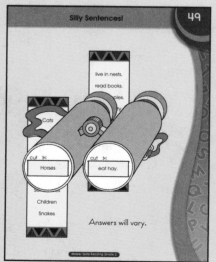

live in nests.
read books.
...ples.
Cats
cut ✂
Horses
cut ✂
eat hay.
...
Children
Snakes

Answers will vary.

49

51 — Synonyms

Words that mean the same or nearly the same are called **synonyms**.

Directions: Read the sentence that tells about the picture. Draw a circle around the word that means the same as the bold word.

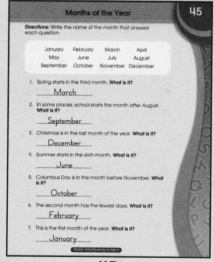

The child is **unhappy**.
(sad) hungry

The flowers are **lovely**.
(pretty) green

The baby was very **tired**.
(sleepy) hurt

The **funny** clown made us laugh.
(silly) glad

The ladybug is so **tiny**.
(small) red

We saw a **scary** tiger.
(frightening) ugly

51

52 — Antonyms

Words that mean the opposite are called **antonyms**.

Directions: Read the sentence. Write the word from the word box that means the opposite of the **bold** word.

bottom	outside	black	summer	after
light	sister	clean	last	evening

1. Lisa has a new baby **brother**. — sister
2. The class went **inside** for recess. — outside
3. There is a **white** car in the driveway. — black
4. We went to the park **before** dinner. — after
5. Joe's puppy is **dirty**. — clean
6. My name is at the **top** of the list. — bottom
7. I like to play outside in the **winter**. — summer
8. I like to take walks in the **morning**. — evening
9. The sky was **dark** after the storm. — light
10. Our team is in **first** place. — last

Master Skills Reading Grade 2

52

53 — Antonyms and Synonyms

Directions: Find the synonyms and antonyms in the puzzle. Words can be up, down, across, or diagonal.

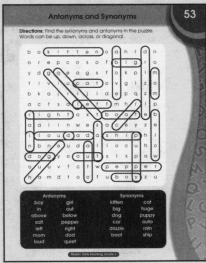

Antonyms		Synonyms	
boy	girl	kitten	cat
in	out	big	huge
above	below	dog	puppy
salt	pepper	car	auto
left	right	drizzle	rain
mom	dad	boat	ship
loud	quiet		

Master Skills Reading Grade 2

53

54 — Classifying

Classifying is putting similar things into groups.

Directions: Write each word from the word box on the correct line.

policeman	baby	whale	family	grandfather
uncle	goose	fox	kangaroo	donkey

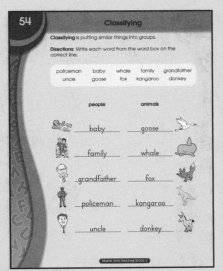

people

baby
family
grandfather
policeman
uncle

animals

goose
whale
fox
kangaroo
donkey

Master Skills Reading Grade 2

54

55 — Classifying

Living things need air, food, and water to live. **Non-living** things are not alive.

Directions: Cut out the words on the bottom. Glue each word in the correct column.

Living	Non-living
horse	camera
flower	shoe
dog	chair
tree	car
ant	book
boy	bread

Master Skills Reading Grade 2

55

57 — Classifying

Directions: Read the sentences. Write the words from the word box where they belong.

bush	rocket	cake	thunder	bicycle	danger
airplane	wind	candy	rain	car	grass
stop	truck	poison	flower	pie	bird

1. These things taste sweet.
   cake candy pie
2. These things come when it storms.
   wind thunder rain
3. These things have wheels.
   car truck bicycle
4. These are words you see on signs.
   stop poison danger
5. These things can fly.
   rocket bird airplane
6. These things grow in the ground.
   flower grass bush

Master Skills Reading Grade 2

57

58 — Classifying

Directions: The words in each box form a group. Choose the word from the word box that describes each group and write it on the line.

clothes	family	noises	colors	flowers
fruits	animals	coins	toys	

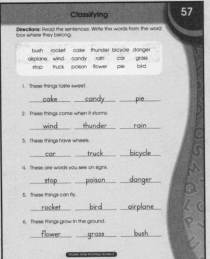

rose	crash	mother
buttercup	bang	father
tulip	ring	sister
daisy	pop	brother
flowers	**noises**	**family**

puzzle	green	grapes
wagon	purple	orange
blocks	blue	apple
doll	red	plum
toys	**colors**	**fruit**

shirt	dime	dog
socks	penny	horse
dress	nickel	elephant
coat	quarter	moose
clothes	**coins**	**animals**

Master Skills Reading Grade 2

58

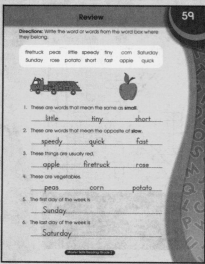

Review

Directions: Write the word or words from the word box where they belong.

firetruck peas little speedy tiny corn Saturday
Sunday rose potato short fast apple quick

1. These are words that mean the same as **small**.
   little   tiny   short

2. These are words that mean the opposite of **slow**.
   speedy   quick   fast

3. These things are usually red.
   apple   firetruck   rose

4. These are vegetables.
   peas   corn   potato

5. The first day of the week is
   Sunday

6. The last day of the week is
   Saturday

59

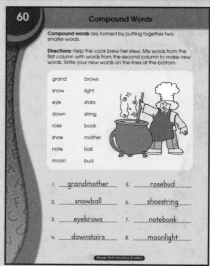

Compound Words

Compound words are formed by putting together two smaller words.

Directions: Help the cook brew her stew. Mix words from the first column with words from the second column to make new words. Write your new words on the lines at the bottom.

grand	brows
snow	light
eye	stairs
down	string
rose	book
shoe	mother
note	ball
moon	bud

1. grandmother
2. snowball
3. eyebrows
4. downstairs
5. rosebud
6. shoestring
7. notebook
8. moonlight

60

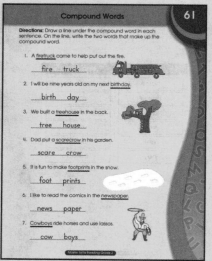

Compound Words

Directions: Draw a line under the compound word in each sentence. On the line, write the two words that make up the compound word.

1. A firetruck came to help put out the fire.
   fire   truck

2. I will be nine years old on my next birthday.
   birth   day

3. We built a treehouse in the back.
   tree   house

4. Dad put a scarecrow in his garden.
   scare   crow

5. It is fun to make footprints in the snow.
   foot   prints

6. I like to read the comics in the newspaper.
   news   paper

7. Cowboys ride horses and use lassos.
   cow   boys

61

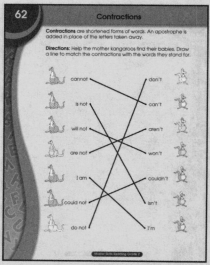

Contractions

Contractions are shortened forms of words. An apostrophe is added in place of the letters taken away.

Directions: Help the mother kangaroos find their babies. Draw a line to match the contractions with the words they stand for.

cannot — can't
is not — isn't
will not — won't
are not — aren't
I am — I'm
could not — couldn't
do not — don't

62

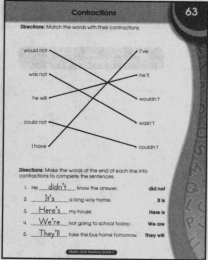

Contractions

Directions: Match the words with their contractions.

would not — wouldn't
was not — wasn't
he will — he'll
could not — couldn't
I have — I've

Directions: Make the words at the end of each line into contractions to complete the sentences.

1. He didn't know the answer.   did not
2. It's a long way home.   It is
3. Here's my house.   Here is
4. We're not going to school today.   We are
5. They'll take the bus home tomorrow.   They will

63

Contractions

Directions: Write your own contractions in each column below.

Contractions with not	Contractions with will	Contractions with have
	Answers will vary.	

Challenge: Write the two words that formed each contraction.

64

65 — Contractions

Directions: Cut out the two words and put them together to show what two words make the contraction. Glue them over the contraction.

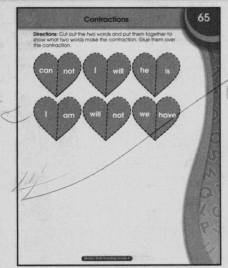

can / not	I / will	he / is
I / am	will / not	we / have

65

67 — Similes

A **simile** is a figure of speech that compares two different things. The words **like** or **as** are used in similes.

Directions: Draw a line to the picture that goes with each set of words.

as hard as a
as hungry as a
as quiet as a
as soft as a
as easy as
as light as a
as tiny as an

67

68 — Syllables

One way to help you read a word you don't know is to divide it into parts called **syllables**. Every syllable has a vowel sound.

straw•ber•ry

Directions: Say the words. Write the number of syllables.

bird	1	rabbit	2
apple	2	elephant	3
balloon	2	family	3
basketball	3	fence	1
breakfast	2	ladder	2
block	1	open	2
candy	2	puddle	2
popcorn	2	Saturday	3
understand	3	butterfly	3

68

69 — Syllables

When a double consonant is used in the middle of a word, the word can usually be divided between the consonants.

Directions: Look at the words in the word box. Divide each word into two syllables. Leave space between each syllable. The first one is done for you.

butter	puppy	kitten	yellow
dinner	chatter	ladder	happy
pillow	letter	mitten	summer

but ter	chat ter	mit ten
din ner	let ter	yel low
pil low	kit ten	hap py
pup py	lad der	sum mer

Many words are divided between two consonants that are not alike.

Directions: Look at the words in the word box. Divide each word into two syllables. The first one is done for you.

window	doctor	number	carpet
mister	winter	pencil	candle
barber	sister	picture	under

win dow	win ter	pic ture
mis ter	sis ter	car pet
bar ber	num ber	can dle
doc tor	pen cil	un der

69

70 — Syllables

Directions: Write 1 or 2 on the line to tell how many syllables are in each word. If the word has two syllables, draw a line between the syllables. **Example:** sup|per

dog	1	timber	2
bedroom	2	cat	1
slipper	2	street	1
tree	1	chalk	1
batter	2	blanket	2
chair	1	marker	2
fish	1	brush	1
master	2	rabbit	2

70

71 — Review

Directions: Circle the word that fits best into each sentence.

1. It is fun to build castles in a ___.
   (sandbox)   hatbox
2. You carry your books in your ___.
   (bookbag)   lunchbag
3. Fall is the best season for playing ___.
   (football)   footprint
4. We ___ ready when our ride came.
   (weren't)   he'll
5. Why ___ my bike be fixed?
   (couldn't)   I'm
6. We ___ see over your head.
   (can't)   isn't
7. This test is as easy as ___.
   (pie)   pillow
8. The baby feels as light as a ___.
   (feather)   tree

Directions: Count the syllables in each word. Write the number on the line. The first one is done for you.

strawberry	3	toenail	2
missing	2	broken	2
understand	3	turtle	2
circle	2	green	1

71

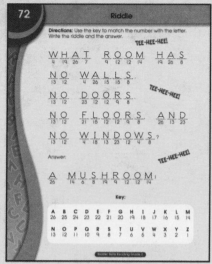

72 — Riddle

Directions: Use the key to match the number with the letter. Write the riddle and the answer.

TEE-HEE-HEE!

WHAT ROOM HAS
4 19 26 7   9 12 12 14   19 26 8

NO WALLS.
13 12   4 26 15 15 8

TEE-HEE-HEE!

NO DOORS.
13 12   23 12 12 9 8

NO FLOORS AND
13 12   21 15 12 12 9 8   26 13 23

NO WINDOWS?
13 12   4 18 13 23 12 4 8

Answer:

TEE-HEE-HEE!

A MUSHROOM.
26   14 6 8 19 9 12 12 14

Key:

A	B	C	D	E	F	G	H	I	J	K	L	M
26	25	24	23	22	21	20	19	18	17	16	15	14

N	O	P	Q	R	S	T	U	V	W	X	Y	Z
13	12	11	10	9	8	7	6	5	4	3	2	1

Master Skills Reading Grade 2

72

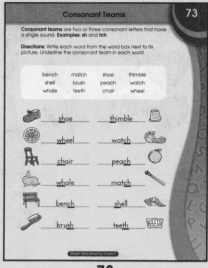

73 — Consonant Teams

Consonant teams are two or three consonant letters that have a single sound. **Examples:** sh and tch

Directions: Write each word from the word box next to its picture. Underline the consonant team in each word.

bench   match   shoe   thimble
shell   brush   peach   watch
whale   teeth   chair   wheel

shoe   thimble
wheel   watch
chair   peach
whale   match
bench   shell
brush   teeth

Master Skills Reading Grade 2

73

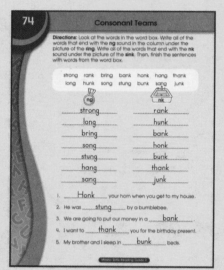

74 — Consonant Teams

Directions: Look at the words in the word box. Write all of the words that end with the **ng** sound in the column under the picture of the **ring**. Write all of the words that end with the **nk** sound under the picture of the **sink**. Then, finish the sentences with words from the word box.

strong   rank   bring   bank   honk   hang   thank
long   hunk   song   stung   bunk   sang   junk

ng / **nk**

strong	rank
long	hunk
bring	bank
song	honk
stung	bunk
hang	thank
sang	junk

1. __Honk__ your horn when you get to my house.
2. He was __stung__ by a bumblebee.
3. We are going to put our money in a __bank__.
4. I want to __thank__ you for the birthday present.
5. My brother and I sleep in __bunk__ beds.

Master Skills Reading Grade 2

74

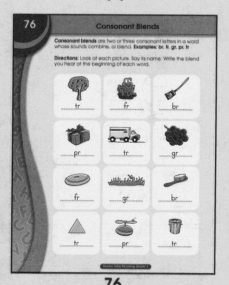

75 — Consonant Teams

Directions: Write a word from the word box to finish each sentence. Circle the consonant teams in your words.

trash   splash   chain   shut   chicken
catch   ship   when   patch   which

1. My __chicken__ won't lay eggs.
2. I put a __chain__ on my bicycle so nobody can take it.
3. We watched the big __ship__ dock and let off its passengers.
4. It is my job to take out the __trash__.
5. I have to wear a __patch__ over my eye until it is better.
6. The baby likes to __splash__ in the bathtub.
7. Can you __catch__ the ball with one hand?
8. Please __shut__ the windows before it rains.
9. __When__ are we going to leave for school?
10. I don't know __which__ of these books is mine.

Master Skills Reading Grade 2

75

76 — Consonant Blends

Consonant blends are two or three consonant letters in a word whose sounds combine, or blend. **Examples:** br, fr, gr, pr, tr

Directions: Look at each picture. Say its name. Write the blend you hear at the beginning of each word.

tr   fr   br
pr   tr   gr
fr   gr   br
tr   pr   tr

Master Skills Reading Grade 2

76

77 — Consonant Blends

Directions: Write a word from the word box to answer each riddle.

clock   glass   blow   climb   slipper
sleep   gloves   clap   blocks   flashlight

1. You need me when the lights go out. **What am I?** — flashlight
2. People use me to tell the time. **What am I?** — clock
3. You put me on your hands in the winter to keep them warm. **What am I?** — gloves
4. Cinderella lost one like me at midnight. **What am I?** — slipper
5. This is what you do with your hands when you are pleased. **What is it?** — clap
6. You can do this with a whistle or with bubble gum. **What is it?** — blow
7. These are what you might use to build a castle when you are playing. **What are they?** — blocks
8. You do this to get to the top of a hill. **What is it?** — climb
9. This is what you use to drink water or milk. **What is it?** — glass
10. You do this at night with your eyes closed. **What is it?** — sleep

Master Skills Reading Grade 2

77

78 — Consonant Blends

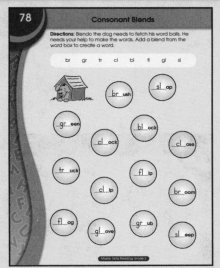

Directions: Blendo the dog needs to fetch his word balls. He needs your help to make the words. Add a blend from the word box to create a word.

br   gr   tr   cl   bl   fl   gl   sl

- br**ush**
- sl**ap**
- gr**een**
- bl**ock**
- cl**ock**
- cl**ose**
- tr**uck**
- fl**ip**
- cl**ip**
- br**oom**
- fl**og**
- gl**ove**
- gr**ub**
- sl**eep**

78

79 — Consonant Teams

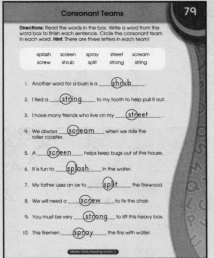

Directions: Read the words in the box. Write a word from the word box to finish each sentence. Circle the consonant team in each word. **Hint:** There are three letters in each team!

splash   screen   spray   street   scream
screw   shrub   split   strong   string

1. Another word for a bush is a **shrub** .
2. I tied a **string** to my tooth to help pull it out.
3. I have many friends who live on my **street** .
4. We always **scream** when we ride the roller coaster.
5. A **screen** helps keep bugs out of the house.
6. It is fun to **splash** in the water.
7. My father uses an ax to **split** the firewood.
8. We will need a **screw** to fix the chair.
9. You must be very **strong** to lift this heavy box.
10. The firemen **spray** the fire with water.

79

80 — Silent Letters

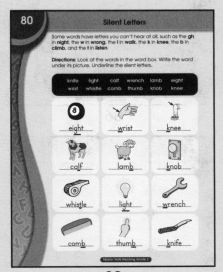

Some words have letters you can't hear at all, such as the **gh** in **night**, the **w** in **wrong**, the **l** in **walk**, the **k** in **knee**, the **b** in **climb**, and the **t** in **listen**.

Directions: Look at the words in the word box. Write the word under its picture. Underline the silent letters.

knife   light   calf   wrench   lamb   eight
wrist   whistle   comb   thumb   knob   knee

- eight
- wrist
- knee
- calf
- lamb
- knob
- whistle
- light
- wrench
- comb
- thumb
- knife

80

81 — Review

Directions: Read the story. Circle the consonant teams (two or three letters) and silent letters in the underlined words. Be sure to check for more than one team in a word! The first one is done for you.

One day last Spring my family went on a picnic. My father picked out a pretty spot next to a stream. While my brother and I climbed a tree, my mother spread out a sheet and placed the food on it. But before we could eat, a skunk walked out of the woods! Mother screamed and scared the skunk. It sprayed us with a terrible smell! Now, we think it is a funny story. But that day, we ran!

Directions: Write the words with three-letter blends on the lines.

Spring   stream   spread   screamed   sprayed

81

82 — Riddle

Directions: Use the key to match the number with the letter. Write the riddle and the answer.

WHY ARE FISH
4 19 2   26 19 22   21 18 8 19

SMARTER THAN
8 14 26 9 7 22 9   7 19 26 13

BIRDS?
25 18 9 23 8

Answer:

BECAUSE THEY
25 22 24 26 6 8 22   7 19 22 2

LIVE IN
15 18 13 22   18 13

SCHOOLS
8 24 19 12 12 15 8

Key:

A	B	C	D	E	F	G	H	I	J	K	L	M
26	25	24	23	22	21	20	19	18	17	16	15	14

N	O	P	Q	R	S	T	U	V	W	X	Y	Z
13	12	11	10	9	8	7	6	5	4	3	2	1

82

83 — Alphabetical Order

Directions: Cut out the scoops of ice cream on the bottom. Glue them on the cones in alphabetical order.

apple   dog   frost   house
lemon   ring   truck

83

Answer Key

85 — Plurals

Plurals are words that mean more than one. You usually add an **s** or **es** to the word. In some words ending in **y**, the **y** changes to an **i** before adding **es**. For example, **baby** changes to **babies.**

Directions: Look at the following lists of plural words. Write the word that means one next to it. The first one is done for you.

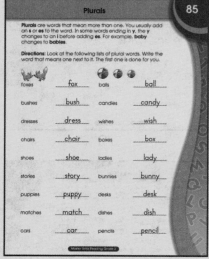

foxes	fox	balls	ball
bushes	bush	candies	candy
dresses	dress	wishes	wish
chairs	chair	boxes	box
shoes	shoe	ladies	lady
stories	story	bunnies	bunny
puppies	puppy	desks	desk
matches	match	dishes	dish
cars	car	pencils	pencil

Master Skills Reading Grade 2

85

86 — Plurals

Directions: Circle the word that completes the sentence.

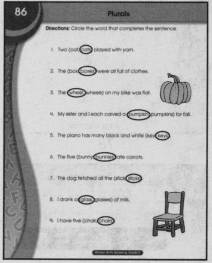

1. Two (cat, **cats**) played with yarn.
2. The (box, **boxes**) were all full of clothes.
3. The (**wheel**, wheels) on my bike was flat.
4. My sister and I each carved a (**pumpkin**, pumpkins) for fall.
5. The piano has many black and white (keys, **keys**).
6. The five (bunny, **bunnies**) ate carrots.
7. The dog fetched all the (stick, **sticks**).
8. I drank a (**glass**, glasses) of milk.
9. I have five (chair, **chairs**).

Master Skills Reading Grade 2

86

87 — Suffixes

A **suffix** is a syllable added to the end of a word which changes its meaning, as in small, smaller, smallest. The word you start with is called the **root word.** Some root words change their spelling before adding **er** and **est. Example:** in the word **big,** another **g** is added to make the words bigger and biggest. In the word **pretty,** the **y** changes to an **i** to make the words prettier and prettiest.

Directions: Use words from the word box to help you add **er** and **est** to the root words.

prettier	happier	luckiest	busiest	tinier
luckier	silliest	greener	madder	busier
prettiest	funnier	tiniest	happiest	bigger
biggest	greenest	sillier	maddest	funniest

	er	est
happy	happier	happiest
busy	busier	busiest
tiny	tinier	tiniest
pretty	prettier	prettiest
lucky	luckier	luckiest
big	bigger	biggest
silly	sillier	silliest
green	greener	greenest
mad	madder	maddest
funny	funnier	funniest

Master Skills Reading Grade 2

87

88 — Suffixes

Adding **ing** to a word means that it is happening now. Adding **ed** to a word means it happened in the past.

Directions: Look at the words in the word box. Underline the root word in each one. Write a word to complete each sentence.

snowing	wished	played	looking	crying
talking	walked	eating	going	doing

1. We like to play. We **played** yesterday.
2. Is that snow? Yes, it is **snowing**.
3. Do you want to go with me? No, I am **going** with my friend.
4. The baby will cry if we leave. The baby is **crying**.
5. We will walk home from school. We **walked** to school this morning.
6. Did you wish for a new bike? Yes, I **wished** for one.
7. Who is going to do it while we are away? I am **doing** it.
8. Did you talk to your friend? Yes, we are **talking** now.
9. Will you look at my book? I am **looking** at it now.
10. I like to eat pizza. We are **eating** it today.

Master Skills Reading Grade 2

88

89 — Suffixes

Directions: Write a word from the word box next to its root word.

| coming | running | sitting | lived | rained |
| swimming | visited | carried | racing | hurried |

run	running	come	coming
live	lived	carry	carried
hurry	hurried	race	racing
swim	swimming	rain	rained
visit	visited	sit	sitting

Directions: Write a word from the word box to finish each sentence.

1. I ___visited___ my grandmother during vacation.
2. Mary went ___swimming___ at the lake with her cousin.
3. Jim ___carried___ the heavy package for his mother.
4. It ___rained___ and stormed all weekend.
5. Cars go very fast when they are ___racing___.

Master Skills Reading Grade 2

89

90 — Suffixes

Directions: Add one of the endings in the box to each root word. Write the correct form of the word to finish each sentence.

| ed | ing |

1. When my dog was a puppy, he often ___chewed___ on old shoes and slippers. **chew**
2. When we saw the cat, it was ___climbing___ a tree. **climb**
3. We ___crossed___ the street to catch the bus. **cross**
4. Mike was ___walking___ in the rain. **walk**
5. A tiny baby is usually either ___eating___ or sleeping. **eat**
6. I ___asked___ David to show me his kitten. **ask**
7. The children were ___playing___ ball in the yard. **play**
8. A big dog ___barked___ at us when we walked by. **bark**
9. I ___hooked___ a fish with my fishing pole. **hook**

Master Skills Reading Grade 2

90

91 — Suffixes

Word families have the same root word in common.

Example: play
plays
played
playing

Directions: Add **s**, **ed**, and **ing** to each root word to create word families.

work	talk	bark
works	talks	barks
worked	talked	barked
working	talking	barking

walk	cook	jump
walks	cooks	jumps
walked	cooked	jumped
walking	cooking	jumping

Master Skills Reading Grade 2

91

92 — Suffixes

A **suffix** is a syllable that is added at the end of a word to change its meaning.

Directions: Add the suffixes to the root word to make new words. Then, use your new words to complete the sentences.

help + ful =	helpful
care + less =	careless
build + er =	builder
talk + ed =	talked
love + ly =	lovely
loud + er =	louder

1. My mother ___talked___ to my teacher about my homework.
2. The radio was ___louder___ than the television.
3. Sally is always ___helpful___ to her mother.
4. A ___builder___ put a new garage on our house.
5. The flowers are ___lovely___.
6. It is ___careless___ to cross the street without looking both ways.

Master Skills Reading Grade 2

92

93 Suffixes

Directions: Read the story. Underline the words that end with **est**, **ed**, or **ing**. On the lines below, write the root words for each word you underlined.

The <u>funniest</u> book I ever read was about a girl <u>named</u> Nan. Nan did everything backward. She even <u>spelled</u> her name backward. Nan slept in the day and <u>played</u> at night. She <u>dried</u> her hair before <u>washing</u> it. She <u>turned</u> on the light after she <u>finished</u> her book—which she read from the back to the front! When it rained, Nan <u>waited</u> until she was inside before opening her umbrella. She even <u>walked</u> backward. The <u>silliest</u> part: The only thing Nan did forward was back up!

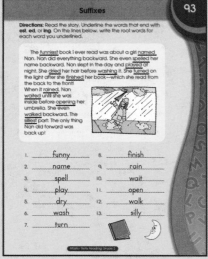

1. _funny_   8. _finish_
2. _name_   9. _rain_
3. _spell_   10. _wait_
4. _play_   11. _open_
5. _dry_   12. _walk_
6. _wash_   13. _silly_
7. _turn_

94 Review

Directions: Read the word in bold in each sentence and circle each suffix. Write the root word on the line. Remember, some root words are changed when an ending is added.

Example: silli**ness** → silly

1. Sue and Tim were **danc**(ing) at the party.   _dance_
2. The children were **care**(ful) not to play in the street.   _care_
3. We made a mistake and put the door on **back**(ward).   _back_
4. This is the **funni**(est) movie I ever saw.   _funny_
5. A new baby is **help**(less).   _help_
6. I **ask**(ed) Mike to bring his wagon to my house.   _ask_
7. I'm really tired today because I had a **sleep**(less) night.   _sleep_
8. My teacher is **real**(ly) nice.   _real_
9. The book I am **read**(ing) is good.   _read_
10. Everyone wants to find **happi**(ness).   _happy_
11. The game isn't **like**(ly) to end soon.   _like_
12. My plant seems to grow **tall**(er) every day.   _tall_

95 Prefixes

Directions: Read the prefix and its meaning. Add each prefix to a root word to make a new word. Write the new word. Then, finish the sentences using the words you just wrote.

Prefixes	(Meaning)	Root Word	New Word
bi	(two)	cycle	bicycle
dis	(away from)	appear	disappear
ex	(out of)	change	exchange
im	(not)	polite	impolite
in	(within)	side	inside
mis	(wrong)	place	misplace
non	(not)	sense	nonsense
pre	(before)	school	preschool
re	(again)	build	rebuild
un	(not)	happy	unhappy

1. Did you go to ___preschool___ before kindergarten?
2. The magician made the rabbit ___disappear___.
3. Put your things where they belong so you don't ___misplace___ them.
4. Can you ride a ___bicycle___?
5. Do you want to ___exchange___ your shirt for one that fits?

96 Prefixes

Directions: Read the story. Change Unlucky Sam to Lucky Sam by taking the **un** prefix off of the **bold** words.

Unlucky Sam

Sam was **unhappy** about a lot of things in his life. His parents were **uncaring**. His teacher was **unfair**. His big sister was **unkind**. His neighbors were **unfriendly**. He was **unhealthy**, too! How could one boy be as **unlucky** as Sam?

Lucky Sam

Sam was ___happy___ about a lot of things in his life. His parents were ___caring___. His teacher was ___fair___. His big sister was ___kind___. His neighbors were ___friendly___. He was ___healthy___, too! How could one boy be as ___lucky___ as Sam?

97

Prefixes

Directions: Change the meaning of the sentences by adding the prefixes to the **bold** words.

The boy was **lucky** because he guessed the answer **correctly**.
The boy was (un) __unlucky__ because he guessed the
answer (in) __incorrectly__.

When Mary **behaved**, she felt **happy**.
When Mary (mis) __misbehaved__,
she felt (un) __unhappy__.

Mike wore his jacket **buttoned** because the dance was **formal**.
Mike wore his jacket (un) __unbuttoned__ because the
dance was (in) __informal__.

Tim **understood** because he was **familiar** with the book.
Tim (mis) __misunderstood__ because he was
(un) __unfamiliar__ with the book.

Master Skills Reading Grade 2

97

98

Prefixes

Directions: Read the story. Change the story by removing the prefix **re** from the **bold** words. Write the new words in the new story.

Repete is a **rewriter** who has to **redo** every story. He has to **rethink** up the ideas. He has to **rewrite** the sentences. He has to **redraw** the pictures. He even has to **retype** the pages. Who will **repay Repete** for all the work he **redoes**?

__Pete__ is a __writer__ who has to
__do__ every story. He has to __think__
up the ideas. He has to __write__ the sentences.
He has to __draw__ the pictures. He even has to
__type__ the pages. Who will __pay__
__Pete__ for all the work he __does__ ?

Master Skills Reading Grade 2

98

99

Prefixes and Suffixes

Directions: See how many new words you can make by adding prefixes and suffixes to the root words. You can use the prefixes, suffixes, and root words as many times as you like.

Prefixes:

bi   dis   ex   in   im   mis   non   pre   re   un

Root Words:

play   obey   friend   feel   health
polite   kind   thought   cycle   like

Suffixes:

ly   ing   ed   y   ful   ness   less   able   ment

__Answers will vary.__

Master Skills Reading Grade 2

99

100

Prefixes and Suffixes

Directions: See how many words you can find. The words can go up, down, left, right, or diagonal.

unhappy	tricycle	disappoint
excite	impress	misfit
preschool	unsafe	friendly
singing	played	sleepy
likeable	kindness	

Master Skills Reading Grade 2

100

Master Skills Reading Grade 2

Answer Key

101 — Review

Directions: Read each sentence. Look at the words in **bold**. Circle the prefix and write the root word on the line.

1. The **preview** of the movie was funny. ____view____
2. We always drink **nonfat** milk. ____fat____
3. We will have to **reschedule** the trip. ____schedule____
4. Are you tired of **reruns** on television? ____run____
5. I have **outgrown** my new shoes already. ____grown____
6. You must have **misplaced** the papers. ____place____
7. Police **enforce** the laws of the city. ____force____
8. I **disliked** that book. ____like____
9. The boy **distrusted** the big dog. ____trust____
10. Try to **enjoy** yourself at the party. ____joy____
11. Please try to keep the cat **inside** the house. ____side____
12. That song is total **nonsense**! ____sense____
13. We will **replace** any parts that we lost. ____place____
14. Can you help me **unzip** this jacket? ____zip____
15. Let's **rework** today's arithmetic problems. ____work____

Master Skills Reading Grade 2

101

102 — Create-a-Word

Directions: Create words by using letters that are connected. See how many you can make!

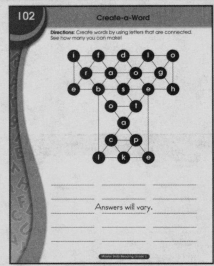

_____
_____
_____
Answers will vary.
_____

Master Skills Reading Grade 2

102

103 — Parts of a Story

Characters are the people or animals in a story.

Directions: Match the familiar stories with the correct characters.

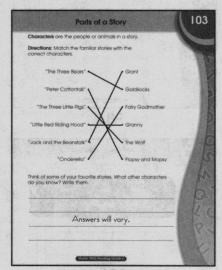

"The Three Bears" — Giant
"Peter Cottontail" — Goldilocks
"The Three Little Pigs" — Fairy Godmother
"Little Red Riding Hood" — Granny
"Jack and the Beanstalk" — The Wolf
"Cinderella" — Flopsy and Mopsy

Think of some of your favorite stories. What other characters do you know? Write them.

_____
_____
Answers will vary.
_____
_____

Master Skills Reading Grade 2

103

104 — Parts of a Book

A book has many parts. The **title** is the name of the book. The **author** is the person who wrote the words. The **illustrator** is the person who drew the pictures. The **table of contents** is located at the beginning to list what is in the book. The **glossary** is a little dictionary in the back to help you with unfamiliar words. Books are often divided into smaller sections of information called **chapters**.

Directions: Look at one of your books. Write the parts you see below.

Answers will vary.

The title of my book is _____

The author is _____

The illustrator is _____

My book has a table of contents. Yes or No

My book has a glossary. Yes or No

My book is divided into chapters. Yes or No

Master Skills Reading Grade 2

104

105 — Following Directions

Here is a recipe for chocolate peanut butter cookies. When you use a recipe, you must follow the directions carefully. The sentences below are not in the correct order.

Directions: Write 1 to show what you would do first. Then, number each step to show the correct sequence.

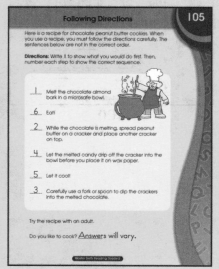

1 — Melt the chocolate almond bark in a microsafe bowl.

6 — Eat!

2 — While the chocolate is melting, spread peanut butter on a cracker and place another cracker on top.

4 — Let the melted candy drip off the cracker into the bowl before you place it on wax paper.

5 — Let it cool!

3 — Carefully use a fork or spoon to dip the crackers into the melted chocolate.

Try the recipe with an adult.

Do you like to cook? ____Answers will vary.____

Master Skills Reading Grade 2

105

Sequencing

Use the comics to help your child practice sequence! Select comics that show a simple sequence, and read the comic strip with your child. Cut the comic strip apart, and challenge your child to rearrange it in the correct order. You could also draw simple pictures in a series, and have your child draw a picture to show what would happen next. Pictures from the family photo album are also fun to sequence. Your child can use the visual clues of growth to help arrange them in sequential order.

Rhymes

Make up silly sentences with your child to practice rhyming skills. For example, "I saw a paper <u>star</u> when I cleaned out the ___." You may also want to say a series of words and have your child tell you which one doesn't rhyme. **Example:** coat, float, dish, goat.

Synonyms

Encourage your child to create more varied and interesting sentences by substituting synonyms for words he or she uses repeatedly. As your child reads his or her writing to you, point out places where a synonym might be used, such as the use of the words **tiny** or **small** instead of **little**.

Riddles

Help your child to create a riddle book. Hold a blank piece of paper lengthwise, and fold over the third on the right. Your child will write the riddle on the exposed part of the paper, with the riddle's answer under the folded over portion. When your child has completed several of these pages, you can staple them together into a book.

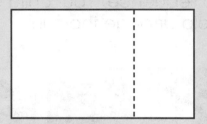 

Short and Long Vowels

Challenge your child to find words in newspapers, magazines, or catalogs that fit a certain phonetic pattern, such as short vowels with the **an** sound or words with the long **e** sound. He or she can cut and glue words with like patterns on separate pieces of paper, and join them to make a phonics book.

Play "Zow!" with your child. Write the word "Zow!" on an index card, and one short vowel word on several additional index cards. Each player draws one card at a time, reading the word on the card. If the card is read correctly, the player gets to keep the card. If the player cannot read the word, the card is returned to the deck. If a player gets the "Zow!" card, he or she gets to take everyone else's card. The player with the most cards wins the game.

Nursery Rhymes

Suggest that your child create a nursery rhyme storybook for a younger child.

Ordinal Numbers

Set up a Family Olympics with your relatives. Make signs, ribbons, etc. that reinforce ordinal numbers, such as first, second, third, etc.

Safety

Call your local poison control center. "Mr. Yuk" books, stickers, and other materials are free of charge, and provide your child important information about poison safety. Also, contact your local fire and police departments. They will often provide your child with free coloring books that help your child learn about fire safety and protection against strangers.